How to Build Unicycles and Artistic Bicycles

Jack Wiley

ISBN-13: 978-1508734260
ISBN-10: 1508734267

CONTENTS

INTRODUCTION   5

1   TOOLS AND MATERIALS   7
Work Areas—Tools—Parts and Materials

2   BASIC CONSTRUCTION TECHNIQUES   10
Assembly and Disassembly—Spoking and Aligning Wheels—
Cutting Frames, Forks, and Stock Materials—Flattening
Tubing—Straightening Fork Prongs—Drilling—Filing and
Grinding—Removing and Installing Chain Links

3   BASIC ASSEMBLIES   15
Fixed-Sprocket Hubs—Crank Sprockets—Unicycle Saddles—
Off-Centered Wheels

4   BUILDING STANDARD UNICYCLES   23
Basic Standard Unicycle—Small-Wheel and Midget—Big
Wheel—Kangaroo Unicycle—Off-Centered Wheel—Pony-
Saddle Unicycle—Standard Unicycle with Handlebars—
Standard Unicycle with Post—Dicycle—Ultimate Wheel—
Ideas for Other Standard Unicycles

5   HANDLEBAR UNITS AND UNIBIKES   47
Handlebar Unit for Standard Unicycle—Handlebar Unit for
Giraffe Unicycle—Break-Apart Units—Unibike

6   BUILDING GIRAFFE UNICYCLES   55
Basic Chain-Driven Giraffe Unicycle—Short Model—Small
Wheel—Tiny Wheel—Big Wheel—Tall Unicycles—Zigzag
Frames—Multi-Wheel Giraffe Unicycles—Tandem Chain-
Driven Unicycles

7   ARTISTIC AND NOVELTY BICYCLES   72
Artistic Bicycles—Novelty Bicycles—Small-Wheel Bicycles—
Off-Centered Wheels—Miniature Bicycles—Other Possibilities

APPENDIX   77
Sources for Unicycles and Parts—Organizations—Publications

INDEX   79

ABOUT THE AUTHOR   81

INTRODUCTION

I have found building unicycles and artistic and novelty bicycles to be a fascinating hobby. I first started building unicycles when I was in the seventh grade. It all started when I purchased a unicycle that had been in a fire. It had belonged to a professional performer. There wasn't much left of it, however. Only a fork and a hub and pedal arms, only enough to tell that it had once been a unicycle. With the help of a man in a bicycle shop, I built the unicycle back up. I mostly watched, but later, after I had learned to ride that first unicycle, I started building unicycles on my own, including not only standard unicycles but also handlebar units, midget unicycles, chain-driven giraffe unicycles, artistic bicycles, and a variety of other related cycles and props.

You can, of course, enjoy unicycling and artistic bicycling without building your own cycles, as detailed in my *The Complete Book of Unicycling: Second Edition* (Infinity Publishing, 2011). It's available from Amazon.com:
http://www.amazon.com/author/ jackwileypublications.

You can purchase manufactured or custom built cycles. However, many people want to not only ride these cycles but also to design and build their own.

Perhaps the most important reason for building your own unicycles and artistic bicycles is to save money. It is often possible to build your own cycles for much less than the cost of manufactured equivalents.

A second reason for building your own is to make unicycles and artistic bicycles of types and designs that are not presently being manufactured. While standard and giraffe unicycles are now being manufactured, these come in limited sizes and designs. If you want something else, you either have to have it custom built or build it yourself. This presently includes handlebar units, big wheel standard unicycles, giraffe unicycles with tiny wheels, giraffe unicycles outside the four to six foot height range, and a variety of multi-wheel and other specialty giraffe unicycles. While artistic bicycles are manufactured in Europe, they are not presently being produced in the United States. Importing them can be an expensive proposition. A practical alternative is to construct your own.

A third reason for building your own cycles is for the fun of doing it yourself. Building unicycles and artistic bicycles can be a rewarding hobby, especially when you get to the point where you are making original designs.

While most people build the cycles for their own use, a few people have set up businesses of building custom cycles for others or manufacturing unicycles.

A variety of materials and component parts can be used for building unicycles and artistic bicycles, including new and used bicycle parts and stock and scrap materials. By using bicycle parts and components, it's possible to do much of the construction work yourself without having to get involved in advanced machining and metal working skills. While most of the construction projects detailed in this book do require at least some brazing and/or welding, you can leave this work to a commercial shop if you don't have the skills and equipment for doing it yourself. The cost is usually reasonable if you have all of the parts shaped and fitted so that only the brazing and/or welding need be done at the commercial shop. In fact, unless you have a thorough knowledge of metals and brazing and welding, this work should be left to a professional. Brazing and welding on unicycles and artistic bicycles must be done properly, as failure could present a safety hazard when using the cycles. My advice is that you leave this work to a professional unless you are certain that you know what you are doing. Whenever you have any doubt whether or not the materials used will be strong enough or can be properly joined together, get professional advice.

This still leaves much that you can do on your own, such as gathering up the required parts, cutting, shaping and fitting them, spoking and aligning wheels, painting, and so on.

Many people do learn to do everything themselves. This involves learning advanced metalworking skills. My advice is that you learn these skills under the guidance of a trained instructor. Skills such as brazing and welding should be thoroughly mastered before attempting them on unicycle or artistic bicycle constructions.

Chapter 1

TOOLS AND MATERIALS

Before going on to basic construction techniques, we will first consider work areas, tools, and materials.

WORK AREAS

A primary consideration is a place to work. If you already have a workshop in your garage or basement, you will probably want to use this. If not, you will need to find a suitable place to set up shop. This should be outside the main living area of your home so that you don't have to worry about spilling oil on the floor or tracking metal particles about the house.

You will need at least one sturdy workbench. Most of the construction work that you do will probably center around the workbench.

The work area does not need to be elaborate, at least not at first. However, as you go along, you will probably want to improve it by adding racks and storage for your tools and materials and supplies.

Good lightning and ventilation are other important considerations.

TOOLS

You will need a basic set of hand tools, including:
- Sets of box and open-end wrenches in metric and inch sizes.
- Pliers.
- Hammers.
- Hacksaw.
- Files.
- Screwdrivers.

- Pipe cutter.

There will probably be other standard hand tools that you will need as you go along. These can be added to your tool collection as needs develop. While you will probably be working primarily with metal and thus require metalworking tools, there will also be times when wood and other materials are used and you will need tools suitable for working with these materials.

One of the most important tools is a heavy-duty utility or metalworking vise, which should be firmly mounted to a workbench.

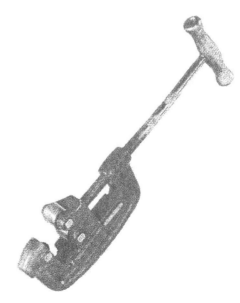

Pipe cutter.

While it is possible to do much of the construction work without any power tools, a few basic power tools will make the work faster and easier. The two most essential power tools, I feel, are a portable electric drill and a bench grinder. A drill press, metal lathe, and other shop tools are useful for advanced metalworking.

You will also need a few special bicycle tools, including:

- Spoke wrench, which is used for tightening and loosening spokes.
- Cone wrenches, which are extra thin open-end wrenches designed especially for use on hub cones and lock nuts.
- Tire levers of small size designed especially for bicycles. Especially handy are the type with a notch that fits over a spoke and holds the tire bead off the rim.
- Chain tool for removing rivets from chains.
- Special tool for removing crank cotters.
- Special wrench and tool for removing and installing cotterless crank arms.

There are also a number of other special tools that are either essential for certain jobs or make them easier that you may want to add to your tool collection if a need develops.

A bicycle maintenance rack, which is a special stand that allow clamping a bicycle in any desired position, will be found useful for many unicycle and artistic bicycle construction tasks.

A number of special tools are available for aligning wheels, but you can improvise here until you are certain that you will be doing enough work to justify the cost of this equipment.

If you intend to do your own brazing and welding, you will need the tools and equipment for this. Many people who build unicycles and artistic bicycles have the brazing and welding done for them. Unless you plan many projects, the cost of the equipment and the time required to learn the skills would probably make doing this work yourself impractical. You can generally have the brazing and welding done quite reasonably at a commercial shop, provided you have everything ready (parts shaped, fitted, and so on) so that only the brazing and welding need be done at the commercial shop.

PARTS AND MATERIALS

In many cases, standard bicycle parts can be used for building the unicycles and artistic bicycles detailed in this book. While new parts can certainly be used, secondhand parts will often serve just about as well, and these can often be purchased at a fraction of the cost of new ones. In some cases, complete used bicycles can be purchased and used for constructing unicycles or converting to artistic bicycles. For many projects, damaged bicycles will provide usable parts. Parts from tricycles, exercise bicycles, and even motorcycles can sometimes be used for making unicycles and artistic bicycles.

Once you have decided on a particular cycle to build, as detailed in later chapters of this book, make a list of the parts that you will need. Parts can often be purchased for low prices at junk and thrift stores, flea markets, garage sales, and bicycle shops. Shop around for the best buys, as prices vary considerably. Some city and county dumps have sale areas, and these often have bicycle parts and even complete cycles in various conditions at low prices. Used bicycles and parts are often advertised in classified ads in newspapers.

Discount stores and auto supply stores are good sources for new bicycle parts. These are often of good or at least adequate quality and are usually priced lower than the same or similar parts purchased at bicycle shops. Of course, when special parts are required, such as a certain length of spokes or a fixed sprocket track hub, a bicycle shop is often your best bet. They often have a large selection of parts on hand and can special order what they don't have in stock.

Mail order and online sources are another possibility (see Appendix). A number of mail order firms feature quality parts at discount prices. Most have illustrated catalogs, for which there is usually a charge, which is often refunded when you make your first purchase.

In some cases, non-bicycle parts can be used. For example, heavy-duty caster wheels are often used for making tiny-wheel unicycles. Large cart or buggy wheels may serve for making big-wheel unicycles.

Stock materials, such as pipe, tubing, rods, and steel stock, can be purchased new or used. As a general rule, I suggest that you use materials of size, thickness, and shape that will be considerably above the minimum strength necessary for the cycle constructed. Allow plenty of margins, especially where failure of a part or material might present a safety hazard.

It is generally best to stick to standard steel bicycle frames and parts and materials if brazing or welding is required. Fortunately, these are generally the least expensive to buy and the most readily available. Factories like standard steel because it is easy to weld with automatic equipment. Aluminum alloy and other light-weight alloys require special equipment and know-how, and even then sound joints can be difficult.

You can also purchase actual unicycle parts, such as saddles and hubs, from some bicycle shops.

Still another possibility is to purchase a used unicycle. Depending on the type and condition, you can repair or restore the unicycle as necessary, use it for parts, or modify it to some other type of unicycle. The availability and price of used unicycles will depend on many factors. I have managed to purchase some at garage sales and thrift stores at very low prices, although they are available in the area where I live only infrequently.

Chapter 2

BASIC CONSTRUCTION TECHNIQUES

Basic construction techniques that are required for making the unicycles and artistic bicycles detailed in later chapters are covered in this chapter. Many people already have the necessary skills. Classes and courses are a good place to learn or improve skills. Adult education classes in metal shop and welding are available in many parts of the United States, often with low, and in some cases nonexistent, fees. These classes are an excellent place for learning skills, and they usually also provide tools and equipment. In some cases you can use the tools and equipment for building a unicycle or artistic bicycle as your class project.

ASSEMBLY AND DISASSEMBLY

Many of the projects detailed in this book require disassembly and/or assembly of bicycles and bicycle components. If you are not familiar with the techniques for doing this, a basic illustrated manual on bicycle repair is suggested. Most public libraries stock one or more of these.

SPOKING AND ALIGNING WHEELS

A number of the projects detailed in this book require spoking and aligning bicycle wheels. A variety of lacing patterns are used on bicycles. Most bicycles use a three or four spoke crossing pattern without interlacing the spokes. In some cases, the spokes are interlaced with the spokes going under instead of over the last spoke in each cross pattern. The lacing patterns are se-

lected to give the bicycle wheels the necessary strength and stiffness at the speeds the bicycle are used.

Three or four spoke lacing patterns without interlacing are typically also used on unicycles and artistic bicycles, although some experts believe that unicycles and artistic bicycles are best spoked without any crossing pattern. The reasoning for this is that, unlike a regular bicycle, unicycles and artistic bicycles are generally ridden at a low speed, and a straight spoking pattern (without crosses) results in the strongest wheel.

In some cases, you will remove the spokes from a wheel so that brazing or welding can be done on the hub. In this case, you can replace the same spokes use new ones of the same length with the same spoking pattern or use spokes of a different length with a different spoking pattern. If you are going to replace spokes with the same lacing pattern, note the lacing pattern and make diagrams as necessary so that you can replace the spokes later in the same pattern. Use a spoke wrench for loosening the nipples on the spokes.

If you have had little or no experience lacing a bicycle wheel, a good place to start is to get an old bicycle wheel. Make a diagram of the spoking pattern. Then remove all spokes from the rim and hub. Then put it all back together again, using the same crossing pattern as was used previously.

Many bicycle repair manuals detail wheel spoking and aligning methods. In

Lacing spokes between hub and rim.

many cases, you will use the same lacing pattern and length of spokes as were used previously. If you use a different size rim or lacing pattern or want to spoke a hub to a rim that has not been spoked before, you will need to get the correct length of spokes and nipple sizes. Charts are available (most bicycle shops have these) that give the correct length of spokes to use with various hub and rim sizes and lacing patterns.

As a general rule, the rim should have the same number of spoke holes as the hub, although there are ways that you can sometimes fudge on this. For example, the rim can have half as many spoke holes as the hub. Then, when lacing the hub, use every other spoke hole.

On most bicycle rims, every other hole is off to one side of the rim. The spokes from one side of the hub go to the corresponding side of the rim.

The spoke holes on opposite sides of the hub flanges are not directly opposite

each other. A hole on one flange is midway between two holes on the opposite flange.

The flanges on some hubs have each spoke hole countersunk on one side. Alternate holes on a flange are countersunk on opposite sides. The spoke head goes on the flush side. The countersunk side is used to reduce stress from the sharp bend in the spoke. Other hubs have the holes countersunk on both sides, allowing the spokes to be positioned in either direction. Alternate spokes on each flange pass through the holes in opposite directions.

The spokes are first passed through the holes in the hub flanges. The threaded ends are then passed through the holes in the rim with the desired crossing pattern and the nipples are installed on the ends and fastened loosely in place.

Once all the spokes are in place, the spokes are ready for tightening and wheel alignment. Bicycle shops usually use a wheel alignment stand for this job. This will also work for giraffe unicycle and artistic bicycle wheels that have standard front or rear bicycle axles. Or you can improvise by using a bicycle fork turned upside down and mounted in a vise. A piece of heavy cardboard is then taped across the fork below the bottom of the rim and two marks are made the rim width and centered between the fork pieces.

Unicycle wheels with other types of axles can be aligned in a similar manner by mounting them in the cycle where they will be used, clamping the cycle in a vise or other suitable support so that the wheel extends upward and is vertical, and taping a piece of cardboard with guide marks across the fork.

Next, align the rim by gradually tightening the spokes with a spoke wrench. Tightening a spoke draws the rim toward the hub and to the side the spoke is on. Loosening the spoke has the opposite effect. Using this logic, continue until the rim is equal distance from the hub center and in alignment. The spokes should be snug, but avoid over tightening them.

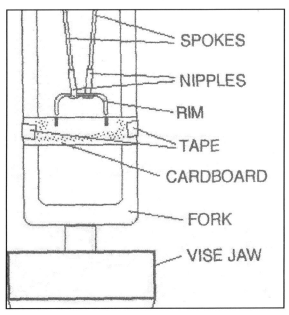

Guide marks are placed on cardboard taped across fork for truing rim.

If spokes of the correct length are used, the threads will not extend through the nipples when they are properly adjusted. If any threads do show, these should be filed off flush with the end of the nipple so that they will not puncture the tube.

Some rear wheels with sprockets are dished to allow space for the sprockets and still have the tire centered. The spokes on the sprocket side are shorter than those used on the other side. The wheel is aligned with the center of the frame where it is mounted rather than midway between the hub flanges.

Spoking a wheel off-center is covered in the next chapter.

CUTTING FRAMES, FORKS, AND STOCK MATERIALS

Many of the construction projects detailed in later chapters require cutting bicycle frames, forks, and stock materials. One way to do this is with a hacksaw. Clamp the frame, fork, or stock metal piece securely in a vise. Make a pattern line. Then make the cut using a hacksaw with a metal

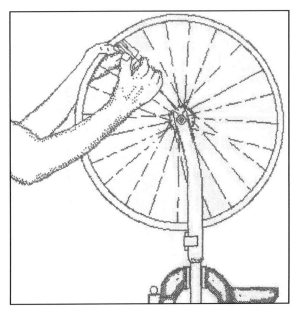

A bicycle fork clamped upside-down in a vise for use as a wheel truing stand.

cutting blade.

When a perpendicular cut is required on round tubing, a pipe cutter can be used. The cutting blades are clamped over the tubing and the device is gradually tightened as it is rotated around the tubing.

FLATTENING TUBING

Bicycle frame and fork tubing, as well as many other types of metal tubing, can be flattened by squeezing the tubing in the jaws of a vise. The degree to which this can be done without fracturing the tubing or weakening the metal depends on the particular metal, the amount of flattening required and other factors.

The tubing can also be flattened by heating it. However, care must be taken so that the temper of the metal is not affected or, if it is, to properly restore it afterwards.

STRAIGHTENING FORK PRONGS

The fork prongs on most bicycles are curved. A number of the projects detailed in this book require straight forks. In some cases, forks can be found that will still be long enough after the curved sections have been cut off. In other cases, it will be necessary to straighten the prongs. This can be done with either flat solid or hollow round or oval prongs. One way to straighten them is to clamp the fork between two blocks of wood in a vise with the curved portion of the fork prongs extending outward. A section of pipe that will just fit over a fork prong is then used to straighten the prong. Work carefully toward the end of the prong, readjusting the fork between the clocks of wood as necessary. If the prongs are of the hollow type, try to avoid making dents in the metal, as these will greatly weaken the tubing.

Fork prongs can also be straightened by heat. However, care must be taken to that the temper of the metal is not affected or, if it is, to properly restore it afterwards.

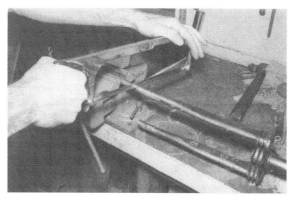

Cutting fork prong with hacksaw.

Straightening a fork prong.

DRILLING

Drilling holes in metal is frequently required. A hand-held portable electric drill will suffice for most of the projects detailed in this book. However, a drill press, if available, will give greater drilling accuracy.

FILING AND GRINDING

Filing and grinding are frequently required for the projects detailed in this book. Most of the filing can be done with flat metal files, but curved and round files are also useful.

A power bench grinder is handy for grinding hard steel cranks, sprockets, and so on. Whenever you use a power bench grinder, use necessary safety devices and wear safety goggles or a face shield.

REMOVING AND INSTALLING CHAIN LINKS

A number of the construction projects require removing and installing chain links, such as for making chains shorter or longer. Since chain breakage on giraffe unicycles and artistic bicycles can present a safety hazard, only heavy duty chain in good condition should be used.

The two basic kinds of chain used on bicycles are wide and narrow. The chain used must fit the sprockets.

Wide chains usually have rollers that are 1/8 inch wide and 1/2 inch pitch (distance between the centers of the rivets). This type of chain is usually used on single speed and three-speed (internal hub geared) bicycles. These chains have a master link for joining the ends.

Narrow chains, used on most derailleur bikes, usually have a 12.7 mm pitch and 2.38 mm width. This type of chain is connected at all links by rivets (master links will not pass through the derailleur mechanisms or fit between the sprockets of derailleur bicycles).

To remove the master link on wide chain, you must have slack in the chain. Locate the master link, which is wider than a normal link. Flex the chain and pry the master link off with a screwdriver. Remove the link posts and backing plate, which slide out as a unit.

To shorten a chain, use a rivet extractor tool (a number of inexpensive models are on the market) to drive out rivet to remove section from chain. Use the master link to rejoin chain ends.

To lengthen a chain, use an additional master link to add a section of chain.

Narrow chains can be shortened and joined in a similar manner, except that a rivet extracting tool is used for removing and installing rivets.

Chapter 3

BASIC ASSEMBLIES

Assemblies that are required for more than one basic type of cycle are detailed in this chapter. Others that are used mainly on only one type of unicycle or artistic bicycle are detailed in later chapters.

FIXED-SPROCKET HUBS

A number of the projects detailed in this book require sprockets that are mounted solid (with no freewheeling) to the hubs. One possibility is to use a track racing bicycle hub of the type shown. This hub has a direct drive. The sprocket threads on and is secured with a lock nut. These hubs are available from bicycle shops and mail-order supply firms. Similar hubs manufactured for giraffe unicycles are also available.

A problem with this type of hub is that the sprockets tend to slip when the pedaling direction is reversed. This usually isn't much of a problem on track bicycles where all the pedaling is done in one direction, which serves to further tighten the sprocket, but problems are sometimes encountered when these hubs are used on chain-driven unicycles and artistic bicycles that are pedaled both forward and backward. In spite of the lock nuts that thread on in the opposite direction to the sprocket threads, these sprockets sometimes work loose. On giraffe unicycles, the sprockets are sometimes positioned on the left side, opposite that of a regular bicycle, so that mounting, which is a back pedaling action that usually places the greatest stress on the drive system, tightens the sprocket.

Another possible solution to the slipping problem is to tack weld the sprocket in place, but this will present problems if you want to remove the sprocket later for installing spokes or other purposes.

Hub with fixed-drive sprocket. The sprocket threads on and is secured by a lock nut.

Fixed-drive hubs are also available with sprockets on both sides. By using dual chain drives, the slipping problem is reduced or eliminated. However, the construction is somewhat more complicated and expensive.

It is also possible to convert a free-wheeling hub of the single-speed coaster brake type to a fixed-drive model. Select a hub assembly that has the type of sprocket that is attached by means of a snap ring. The sprocket itself has three lugs, which fit in notches on the drive screw. This arrangement eliminates the problem of the sprocket slipping by unthreading. Use a hub that has the required number of spoke holes for the cycle that you are making.

To convert a hub of this type to a fixed-drive model, first disassemble all parts, including spokes, sprocket snap ring and sprocket, and axle, bearings, and coaster brake assembly. The clutch cone, brake shoes, clutch spring, clutch washers, and inner bearing retainer and bearings are not used in the fixed-sprocket hub.

With the axle, bearings, sprocket and spokes removed, braze or weld the sprock-et spindle, which includes the inside half of the bearing race for the sprocket side of the hub, to the hub shell. The dust cap, sprocket, and snap ring can then be assembled. The sprocket is easy to remove for spoking the hub to the rim. Cut the brake arm as shown to form a spacer for the hub assembly. This can be done by first cutting straight across the brake arm with a hacksaw. Then use a power bench grinder to round off the corners to form a ring. The axle assembly for the fixed-sprocket hub is shown.

Some stationary exercise bicycles have hubs with fixed sprockets secured with snap rings that may be suitable for giraffe unicycles and artistic bicycles.

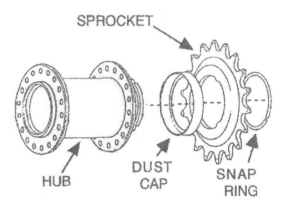

Sprocket lugs fit notches on spindle and is held in place with snap ring.

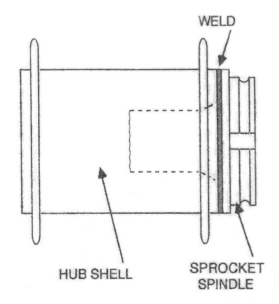

Sprocket spindle is brazed or welded to hub shell.

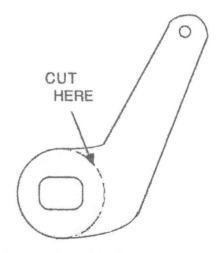

Brake arm is cut to form spacer.

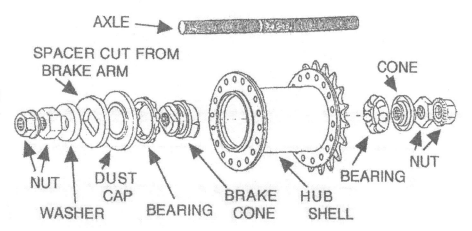

Axle and bearing assembly for fixed-sprocket hub.

CRANK SPROCKETS

A number of the projects detailed in this book require replacing the chain-wheel with a smaller chainwheel or sprocket, often one that matches the sprocket on the wheel hub for a one-to-one gear ratio.

One-Piece Crank Assemblies

For one-piece crank assemblies, the first step is to remove the original chain-wheel from the crank. Small chainwheels that will mount in the same way as a larger chainwheels and fit the same set lug are available that may be small enough for the cycle that you are making. In this case, installation is easy. Position chain-wheel on the crank with crank set lug in hole in chainwheel. Thread stationary cone in place and tighten.

If a sprocket smaller than the smallest chainwheel that will fit is required, a rear sprocket is usually used. Grind off the set

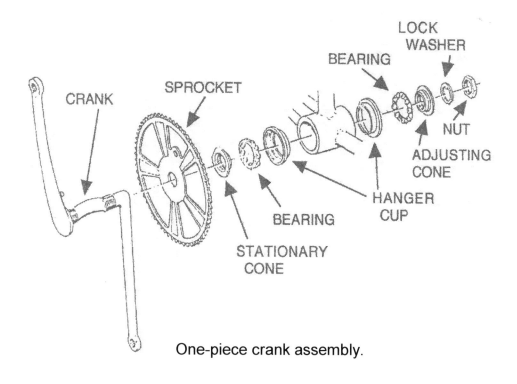

One-piece crank assembly.

Mounting small sprocket to crank.

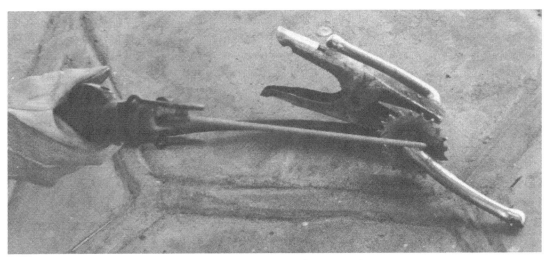

Sprocket is welded to crank.

lug for the chainwheel from the crank. A power bench grinder can be used for this job.

Centering and aligning the sprocket on the crank is extremely important. One way to do this is to fit a thin washer spacer over the cone threads on the sprocket side, then position the small sprocket over the cone threads and tighten the stationary cone against the sprocket.

Before brazing or welding the sprocket in position, test centering and alignment by installing crank back in bottom bracket and spinning it. If centering or alignment is off, this will be apparent. Make required cor-

rections before the sprocket is brazed or welded in place.

Cottered and Cotterless Cranks

If a cottered or cotterless crank assembly is used, it may be possible to obtain a right crank arm of the desired length with a small enough chainwheel already attached.

Some cottered crank arms have the chainwheel splined directly to the crank arm; others have mounting arms splined to the crank arm, with the chainwheel bolted to the mounting arms. The length of the mounting arms vary. In some cases, the arms are short enough that a fairly small

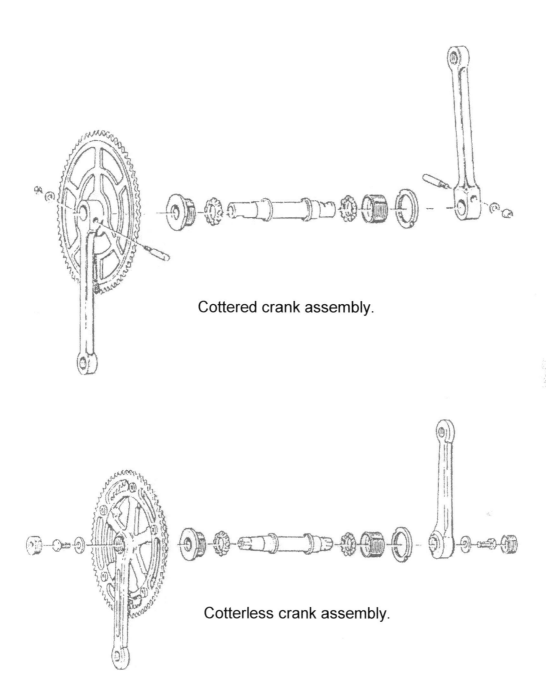

Cottered crank assembly.

Cotterless crank assembly.

chainwheel can be bolted in place. In this case, assembly is easy.

A chainwheel or mounting arms that are splined to the crank arm can be removed by grinding the splined portion of the mounting away. A small sprocket can then be fitted and aligned and centered. The sprocket is then brazed or welded to the crank arm.

Some cotterless crank arms have mounting arms to which the chainwheel is attached; others have the chainwheel attached directly. Brazing or welding a sprocket to an alloy crank arm can be difficult. It is generally easier to bolt a small chainwheel or sprocket to mounting arms, even if this involves cutting the arms to shorter lengths and drilling new mounting holes. Crank arms are made with mounting arms as short as 1 inch, which allows bolting a very small sprocket in place if one can be located with matching holes.

UNICYCLE SADDLES

While standard racing bicycle seats can be used on unicycles, most unicycle riders prefer a long, deeply curved saddle, such as the manufactured models shown. Manufactured unicycle saddles are frequently used on owner-built unicycles. Manufactured unicycle saddles are sometimes available from bicycle shops. They can also be ordered by mail (see Appendix).

Standard bicycle saddles are generally unsatisfactory for use on unicycles. However, it is sometimes possible to modify a standard bicycle seat to make it suitable.

One method is to use a saddle with a full metal base and weld a metal extension to the front of the metal saddle base. Foam rubber padding is then added. Tape the foam rubber in place. Then cover the saddle with desired material. A bicycle saddle modified in this manner for use on a unicycle is shown.

Another possibility is to construct a unicycle saddle base from a block of wood. A pipe or rod that is the correct outside diameter for fitting inside the seat or mounting tube on the unicycle or artistic bicycle is brazed or welded to a flange or metal plate. The saddle base is cut and shaped from wood, then attached to the mounting flange or plate by means of wood screws or bolts. Next, pad the wood with foam rubber and tape it in place. Cover the saddle with desired material.

Manufactured unicycle saddles.

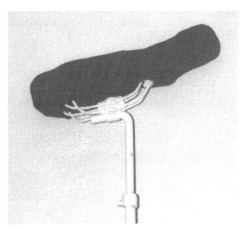

Bicycle saddle modified for use on unicycle.

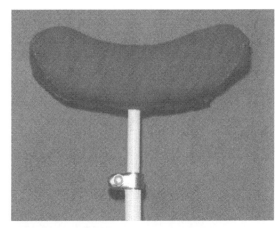

Unicycle saddle with wood base.

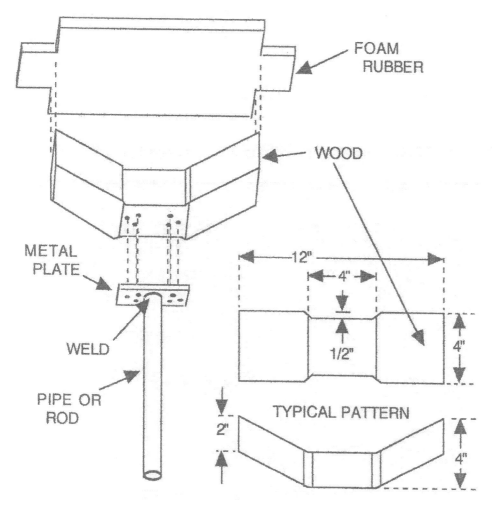

FOAM RUBBER

WOOD

METAL PLATE

WELD

PIPE OR ROD

12"

4"

1/2"

4"

TYPICAL PATTERN

2"

4"

Construction of unicycle saddle with wood base.

Foam rubber is taped in place.

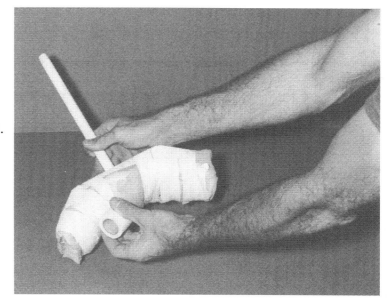

OFF-CENTERED WHEELS

Off-centered wheels are used on novelty unicycles and bicycles detailed in later chapters.

To lace a wheel off-center, you will need varying lengths of spokes. Since it is generally impractical to purchase all of the different lengths of spokes you will need, the usual method is to purchase spokes that are longer than needed. Each spoke is then bent 90 degrees at the desired distance from the rim and passed through a hub spoke hole. The spoke is then bent on around or back in the original direction, as shown. More difficult is to cut the nipple end of each spoke to length, then thread the end with a die.

A wheel can be off-centered any desired amount, provided that there will still be adequate clearance between the wheel and the wheel well and the pedals will have adequate ground clearance. Two inches off center is usually ample to give a good effect.

Before attempting to lace a wheel off-centered, you should first know how to lace a wheel in the normal manner, as detailed in Chapter 2.

Construction of a platform for holding the hub and rim in off-centered position, as shown, will make spoking a wheel off-centered easier. A hole is drilled in the wood base for one end of the hub axle. Prop rim up with blocks as necessary and use nails to hold rim in desired position.

Various crossover patterns can be used. It is helpful to have a regular spoked wheel with the desired lacing pattern to use as a model. When installing spokes in the off-centered wheel, the hub should be twisted like the one that is being used as a model when determining the length for a particular spoke.

When all spokes have been installed in the off-centered wheel, finger tighten all spokes. Then mount the laced wheel tem-porarily back on the cycle where it will be used. Use a spoke wrench for final tightening of spokes. Adjust spokes as necessary to remove side-to-side wobble of rim. Cut and file the ends of any spokes that extend through the nipples. Then install rim liner, tube, and tire to complete the construction of an off-centered wheel.

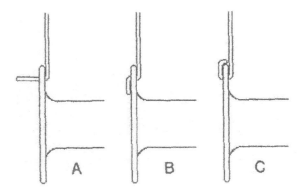

Bending and installing spoke: (A) bend to right angle, (B) make second bend after spoke passes through hole, or (C) make loop in spoke.

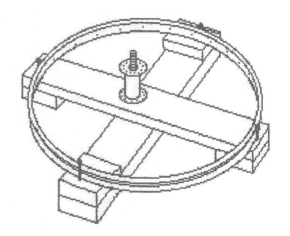

Platform for spoking an off-centered wheel.

Chapter 4

BUILDING STANDARD UNICYCLES

Standard unicycles are defined here as having an axle that is fixed to the wheel hub and pedal arms that are fixed to the axle. The wheel assembly turns freely in bearings that are attached to the fork prongs. The wheel and fork assembly is similar to that used on early penny farthings, and there is considerable evidence that standard unicycles evolved from these cycles. If this is true, the first unicycles probably had large wheels.

The construction of what might be considered a basic standard unicycle with a 20-inch, 24-inch, or 26-inch wheel is detailed first. Most manufactured unicycles are of this type. Standard unicycles with both smaller and larger wheels and a number of

An 1881 catalog illustration of the Standard Columbia penny farthing.

novelty variations, including a number of cycles that are not presently being manufactured, are then covered.

BASIC STANDARD UNICYCLE

The assembly of a basic standard unicycle is shown. The parts required are as follows:

- Complete rear bicycle wheel with coaster brake hub that is the same on both ends or other hub with inside diameter large enough to allow a 5/8-inch axle to pass through it.
- Bicycle fork.
- Saddle-post clamp.
- Saddle post.
- Unicycle saddle.
- Bearings (two required).
- Bearing holders (two required).
- Axle.
- Cottered crank arms, crank pins, washers, and nuts (two of each required) or cotterless crank arms and mounting bolts (two of each required).
- Pedals (two required).

The above parts list makes use of standard bicycle parts. A number of alternative building methods, including substituting stock materials for some of the bicycle parts, are also detailed.

Wheel Assembly

A standard unicycle requires an axle that is solid with the hub. Since the hub is

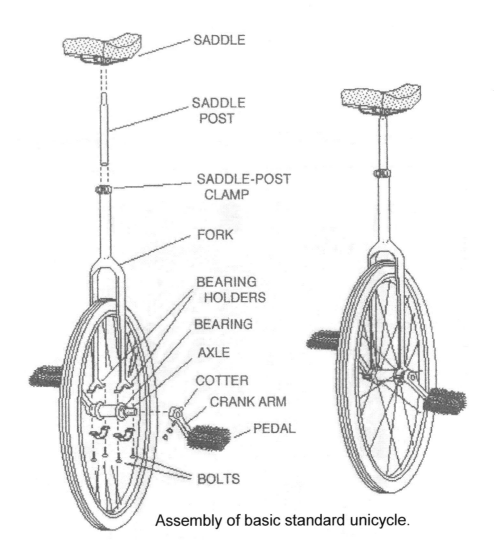

SADDLE

SADDLE
POST

SADDLE-POST
CLAMP

FORK

BEARING
HOLDERS

BEARING

AXLE

COTTER

CRANK ARM

PEDAL

BOLTS

Assembly of basic standard unicycle.

fairly difficult to construct, some builders use a manufactured hub. These are available for either cottered or cotterless crank arms.

For making your own unicycle hub, one possibility for the axle is to use one from a bicycle. In this case, the axle can be either the cottered or cotterless type. For most unicycle assemblies, you will need an axle about 6 inches in length, with about 4-1/2 inches between the crank arms when they are installed on the axle. The bicycle axle needs to be machined down to 5/8-inch or other required diameter to permit the bearings to fit over it. The axle can be this diameter along its entire length or the section that will be inside the hub can be

left at a larger diameter as long as it will fit inside the hub. If you do not have the skill and/or equipment for turning down the axle yourself, you can have this work done for you at a machine shop.

An alternate method is to make an axle for cottered crank arms from 5/8-inch diameter steel axle stock. Diametrically opposite cotter slots are filed or machine in the axle for the crank pins. While this job can be done with a file, you may want to have it done for you at a machine shop. The slots must be made accurately so there will be no play in the crank arms when they are connected to the axle with the cotter pins and the crank arms will line up with each other.

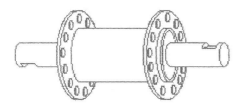

Standard unicycle hub has axle solid with hub.

Axle for cottered cranks.

Axle for cotterless cranks.

There are two main possibilities for adding the spoke flanges to the axle: to join a bicycle hub to the axle or to attach steel washers with spoke holes drilled in them directly to the axle.

For the first method, a coaster brake hub that is identical in size and shape on both ends, not over 2-1/2 inches in length, and has a hole through it that is large enough to take the axle can be used. There are also other hubs, including some front hubs, that will meet these qualifications. In some cases, depending on the length of the axle used, width of bearings, and other factors, you may be able to use a hub that is wider than 2-1/2 inches. The hub should have the same number of spoke holes as the rim you intend to use with it.

The hub assembly is shown. The hub is centered on the axle. One way to do this is to use 5/8-inch washers. Grind the outside of these down until they will just fit inside the ends of the hub. The axle should be in the exact center of the hub with equal lengths extending from each end. The axle and hub are then brazed or welded together to form a single unit.

A hub assembly using steel washers for spoke flanges is shown. To make the hub, select two matching washers that will just slip over the axle with a tight fit. Drill the desired number of spoke holes in the washers. These are usually 1/16-inch diameter holes with the centers 3/16 inch from the outside edges of the washers. Countersink the holes for the bend in the spokes.

The washers are then positioned and lined up on the axle. Braze or weld the washers to the axle to form a single unit.

For either type of hub, the hub can be spoked to the rim at this time or you can wait until the remainder of the unicycle has been constructed. Methods for lacing wheels are detailed in Chapter 2. If the wheel is spoked at this time, final alignment can wait until the wheel assembly is fastened in the unicycle frame to the bearing holders where it is going to be used.

The bearings used should fit snugly over the axle. For example, if a standard

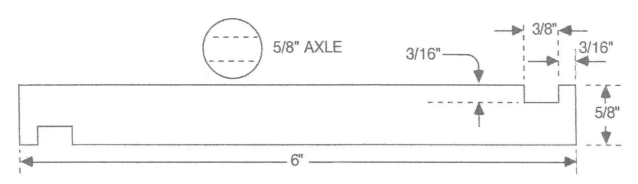

Pattern for making axle from 5/8-inch steel shaft.

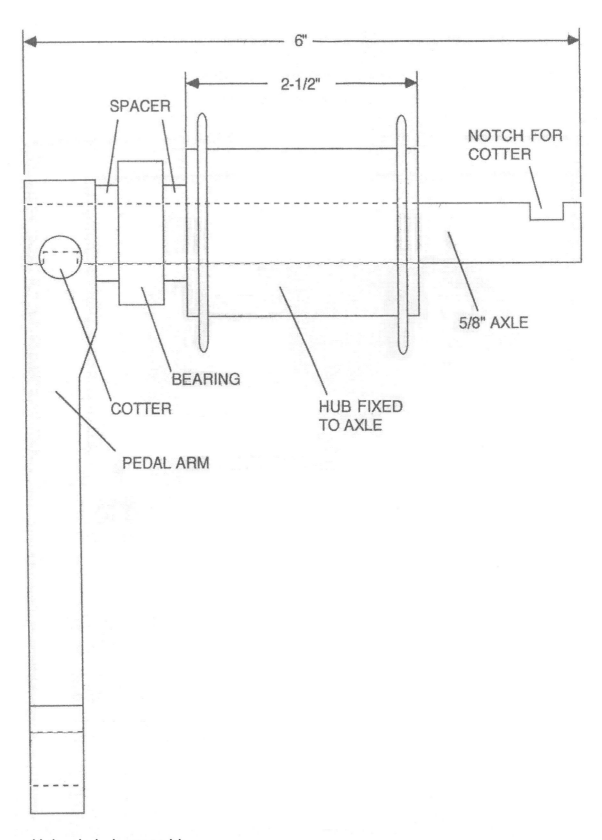

Unicycle hub assembly.

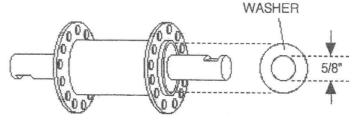

Washers are used as spacers for centering hub to axle.

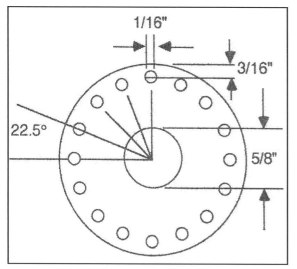

Pattern for drilling steel washers for 32-spoke rim.

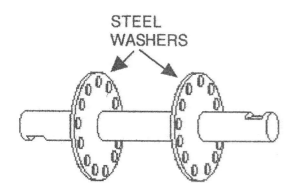

Hub assembly using steel washers for flanges.

5/8-inch axle is used, the bearings should have a 5/8-inch inside diameter. While a variety of bearings can be used, I prefer sealed bearings. These should be heavy-duty bearings, but do not need to be high-speed bearings. As a general rule, tricycle bearings are not sturdy enough for use on a unicycle. Many industrial-type bearings should give good results. One size suitable for many types of holders is 1/2 inch wide and has an outside diameter of 1-1/2 inches.

You can also purchase manufactured unicycle bearings, including those that have grooves for snap rings for one type of mounting to holes in flat unicycle fork prongs (detailed later in this chapter).

When installing the bearings, make sure there will be ample clearance between the fork and the spokes and the fork and crank arms. Add spacers between the hub flanges and bearings and between the bearings and crank arms as required.

Next, install the crank arms. For a 20-inch wheel, I prefer 5-1/2 inch long crank arms; for a 24-inch wheel, 6 inch crank arms; and for a 26-inch wheel, 6-1/2 inch crank arms. However, this is largely a matter of personal preference, and other lengths will also work.

A pair of crank arms can be used if the chainwheel or chainwheel mounting arms is removed from the right crank arm. This can usually be done by grinding. An alternate method is to use two left pedal arms, in which case you will also need to use two left pedals instead of a pair.

After you have completed the unicycle frame, as detailed below in this chapter, you can fasten the wheel assembly in the frame for alignment of the rim. Then remove the wheel assembly from the frame and install rim liner, tub, and tire. A completed wheel assembly is shown.

A completed wheel assembly.

Frame Assembly

Many types of bicycle forks of both the flat steel and hollow variety can be used for unicycles. A fork with straight fork prongs is usually used on unicycles. Most bicycle forks are curved for a caster effect. In some cases, if a long fork is used, it will be possible to cut off all the curved portion of the prongs and still have enough length left. On the completed unicycle, you will need 1/2 inch or more clearance in-between the tire and wheel well.

In other cases, it will be necessary to straighten the curved portions of the prongs to give the required length. Methods for straightening forks are detailed in Chapter 2.

Cut the threaded portion of the fork stem off. Cut a 3/16-inch wide, 1-inch long notch in the fork stem, as shown. Use a saddle post that will just fit inside the fork

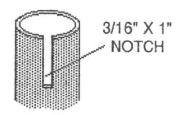

3/16" X 1"
NOTCH

Notch is cut in fork stem.

stem and a standard saddle-post clamp for holding it in place.

An alternate method is to omit the notch and use an expansion-bolt saddle post (available from bicycle supply sources). Both methods allow adjustment of the saddle height.

In some cases, it will be necessary to reinforce the fork stem, such as by adding a section of tubing that will just fit over the fork stem and brazing or welding this in place.

An alternate method for constructing a unicycle frame is to use stock materials instead of a bicycle fork. This is generally more difficult than using a bicycle fork. A typical construction using flat steel stock for the fork pieces with the saddle post bolted to the two fork sections is shown. Unicycle frames can also be constructed from square and round tubing.

There are several possibilities for constructing bearing holders or supports. The purpose of the bearing holders is to support the bearings in a fixed position on the ends of the fork prongs. There should be an easy way to remove the wheel. The bearing holders must fit the bearings used.

One popular type of bearing holders for standard unicycles is the split-block. Two

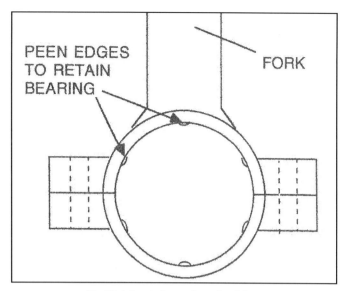

Split-block bearing holder.

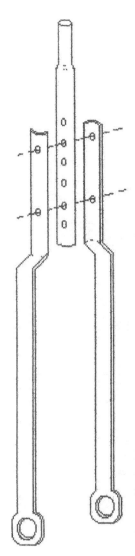

Unicycle frame constructed from flat steel stock.

holders are required for a standard unicycle. These can be purchased from industrial bearing suppliers, or you can construct your own.

Split-block holders can be made from short pieces of pipe that have the same inside diameter as the outside diameter of the bearings. The sections of pipe should be 1/16 inch wider than the bearings. File or grind 3/4-inch pieces of 5/8-inch diameter rod to fit the sides of the pipe section, as shown. Next, clamp the pieces together and

braze or weld the rod pieces to the pipe section. Drill 1/8-inch holes through the centers of the rod sections for securing the sections with bolts and nuts. An alternate method is to drill 3/16 inch holes. Then use a tap to cut threads through the holes.

Next, cut the holders in half. A hacksaw can be used for this job. If the holes were threaded, drill the holes in the bottom or top sections of each holder out to 1/8 inch.

Cut the fork prongs to the desired length. In most cases, there should be at least 1/2 inch clearance between the tire and the wheel well on the completed unicycle. Next, temporarily fasten the bearing holders around a piece of pipe that has the same outside diameter as the bearings with mounting bolts and nuts or bolts alone if you cut threads in the rod sections. The holders should be positioned the same distance apart as the bearings are mounted on the unicycle hub assembly.

It may be necessary to bend the fork prongs outward or inward slightly to fit the width of the bearing holders. Make sure that everything is lined up. Then braze or weld the bearing holders to the ends of the

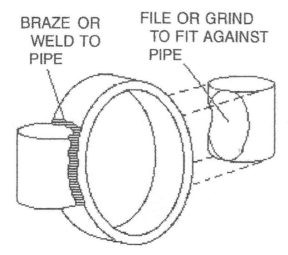

Rods are filed or ground to fit against pipe.

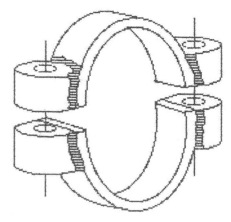

Bearing holder is cut into two sections.

fork prongs. Peen the edges of the bearing supports to retain bearings.

A unicycle fork with split-block holders that was constructed in this manner is shown.

If manufactured split-block bearing holders are used, these can be installed in the same manner. One type of manufactured holder that I have used bolts to a flat plate that is welded on the end of the fork prongs.

Another method for constructing bearing holders is to use saddle-post clamps that will just fit over the bearings when spread apart, as shown. Bent bolts are used to hold the bearings in place. Temporarily mount the bearing holders on a piece of pipe the correct distance apart for the wheel assembly and then braze or weld them to

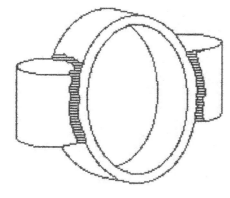

Rods are brazed or welded to pipe.

Split-block bearing holders mounted to pipe.

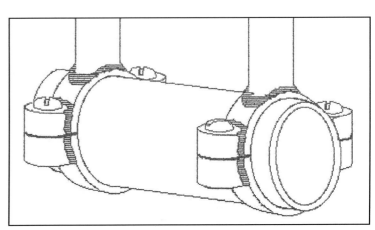

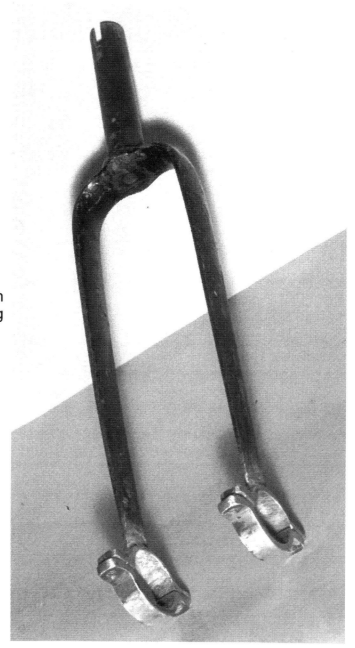

Unicycle fork with split-block bearing holders.

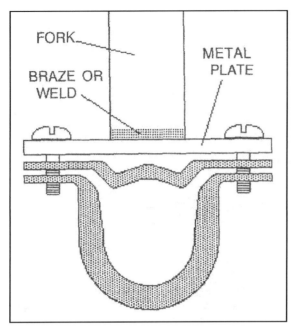

Bearing holder that is bolted to metal plate.

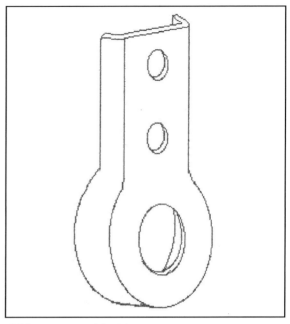

Side-mounted holder.

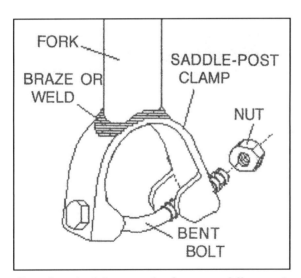

Bearing holder made from saddle-post clamp and bent bolt.

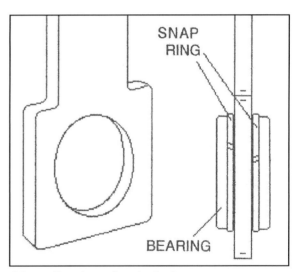

Mounting bearing in hole.

BUILDING STANDARD UNICYCLES

the ends of the fork prongs. I have had good results with this type of bearing holders, which are much easier to make than the split-block type.

Another possibility is to use side mounted bearing holders, similar to those used on tricycles, only of heavier construction. These can be difficult to construct, however.

Still another method, which is popular for forks that are constructed from flat steel stock, is to make tight-fitting holes in the steel stock for the bearings, as shown. Bearings with grooves for snap-in-place retaining rings are then held in place by a retaining ring on each side of the bearing mounting hole.

The unicycle frame can be painted or chrome plated, as desired.

Unicycle Saddle

Unicycle saddles are detailed in Chapter 3. The saddle is either attached directly to the saddle post or held in place by a clamp. The saddle post is held at the desired height in the unicycle frame by means of a saddle-post clamp or, when a split fork made from flat steel stock is used, with mounting bolts. Holes are required for each different height adjustment desired.

Final Assembly

The wheel assembly is attached to the bearing holders. A unicycle that I constructed as detailed above with split-block bearing holders and another with manufactured holders that attach to metal plates welded to the fork prong ends are shown.

Completed standard unicycle with split-block bearing holders.

Completed standard unicycle with manufactured bearing holders bolted to
metal plates on ends of fork prongs.

SMALL-WHEEL AND MIDGET

Standard unicycles can be constructed with smaller wheel sizes than used for the basic standard unicycle described above. Ideally, these should be constructed like the basic standard unicycle detailed above, only with a smaller wheel, shorter pedal arms, and shorter fork prongs. A unicycle of this type that I constructed using saddle-post clamps for bearing holders is shown.

A midget standard unicycle carries the small-wheel concept further by also mak-ing the frame and saddle to a reduced scale. The basic idea is often to construct the smallest possible unicycle that can still be ridden. Again, these are best constructed in the same manner as the basic standard uni-cycle described above, except on a smaller scale.

Another possibility is to construct a midget unicycle from a tricycle wheel. While tricycle wheels generally do not make very good unicycles because of poor strength and precision, the midget unicycle shown was constructed from the sturdiest 10-inch diameter tricycle wheel that I could find, and it has stood up to limited adult use as a novelty part of unicycle acts and demonstrations.

You might also be tempted to construct a tricycle-wheel unicycle for use by a child. However, I don't recommend this. The lack of precision generally make these unicycles more difficult to ride than a regular stand-ard unicycle built on a reduced scale, and the tricycle-wheel unicycle is often an add-ed obstacle for someone who is trying to learn to ride.

Standard unicycle with small wheel.

Tricycle-wheel unicycles do offer the advantage of being simple and inexpensive to construct. The list of parts for the midget unicycle shown is as follows:

- Tricycle-wheel assembly with pedals, bearings, and bearing holders.
- Standard bicycle fork.
- Bolts, washers, and nuts for fastening fork to bearing holders.
- Standard bicycle saddle-post clamp.
- Saddle post of desired length (10-inch long post was used on the unicycle shown).
- Unicycle saddle.

A 10-inch wheel was used on the unicycle shown, but larger or smaller sizes can also be used. Use the sturdiest assembly you can find and make sure that the bearings and holders are in good condition.

The unicycle fork is made by cutting the ends off the prongs of a standard bicycle fork (6 to 8 inches from the wheel well is about right for a 10-inch wheel). The ends of the prongs are flattened in a vise until they are the correct width to fit the bearing holders. The fork prongs are then marked and drilled for connecting the fork to the wheel assembly. The wheel assembly is fastened to the fork with bolts, lock washers, and nuts.

Cut the threaded end off the fork stem and a 3/16-inch wide, 1-inch long notch in the fork stem for the saddle-post clamp.

A 10-inch long saddle post that fit inside the fork stem was used on the unicycle shown. The saddle was constructed with a wood base, as detailed in Chapter 3. However, if desired, a modified bicycle saddle or a manufactured unicycle saddle can be used.

A bicycle saddle-post clamp is used to hold the saddle post at desired height in the fork stem.

The unicycle can be painted as desired.

Tricycle-wheel midget unicycle.

Bearing holders are bolted to fork.

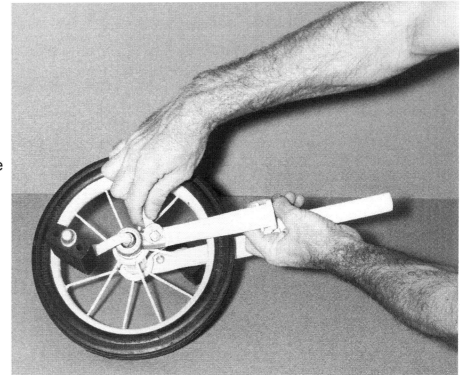

A bicycle saddle-post is used on midget unicycle.

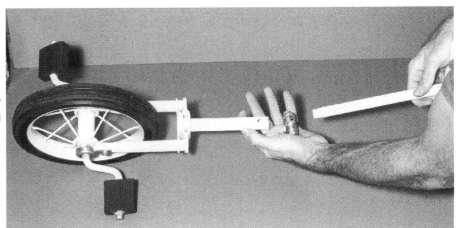

BIG WHEEL

A unicycle with a big wheel is a popular variation of the standard unicycle. Wally Watts of Canada used a unicycle of this type with a 43-inch wheel for an around-the-world unicycle ride, which he completed in 1979. Dave Moore built and Steve Gordon successfully rode a unicycle of this type with a wheel diameter of 73 inches.

It's important that you don't use a wheel that is so large that you won't be

Big-wheel unicycle made from wagon wheel.

able to reach the pedals. Most of the big-wheel unicycle that I have seen have wheels in the 38-inch to 42-inch size range.

The main construction problem is the unavailability of standard parts that can be used for the wheel and frame assembly. One possibility for constructing a large wheel rim is to cut smaller rims and weld two or more of these together to form a larger rim. Another possibility is to use a wooden buggy wheel. Penny farthing wheels can also be used (see Appendix for sources).

The frames for big-wheel unicycles can be constructed from flat steel stock or tubing. A short fork stem is usually used so that the saddle can be mounted close to the wheel, although the length can vary depending on the wheel size and the leg length of the intended rider.

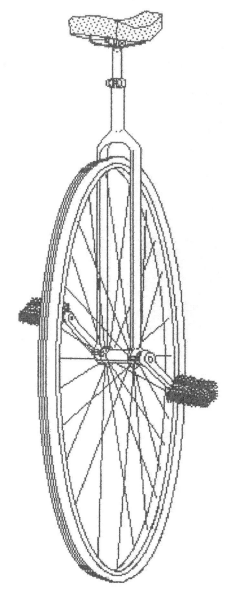

Big-wheel unicycle.

KANGAROO UNICYCLE

A kangaroo unicycle has the crank arms set adjacent to each other. A standard unicycle with cotter-mounted crank arms can be converted to a kangaroo model by removing one crank arm, filing or grinding a cotter-pin notch opposite the original one on the axle, and then installing the crank arm in the new position.

A standard unicycle that has cotterless crank arms is even easier to convert. Remove one of the crank arms (special tools are required to do this), reposition the crank arm in the opposite direction, and then attach the crank arm in new position with the mounting bolt.

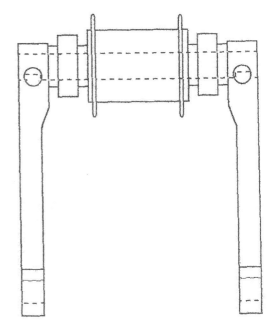

Kangaroo unicycle has crank arms set adjacent to each other.

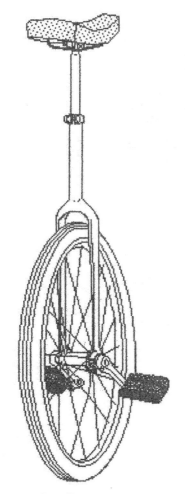

Kangaroo unicycle.

OFF-CENTERED WHEEL

Standard unicycles can be constructed with off-centered wheels. The construction of off-centered wheels is detailed in Chapter 3. If you convert a basic standard unicycle to an off-centered wheel model, it may be necessary to change to a smaller wheel size in order to have adequate clearance under the wheel well. A wheel that is off-centered about 2 inches will usually give a good effect.

PONY-SADDLE UNICYCLE

A pony-saddle unicycle can be constructed by adding a plastic horse from a rocking horse to a standard unicycle. The plastic horses or other animals are often available at secondhand stores for low prices. These can be bolted to a bicycle saddle that has a metal base or a unicycle saddle for mounting them on a unicycle.

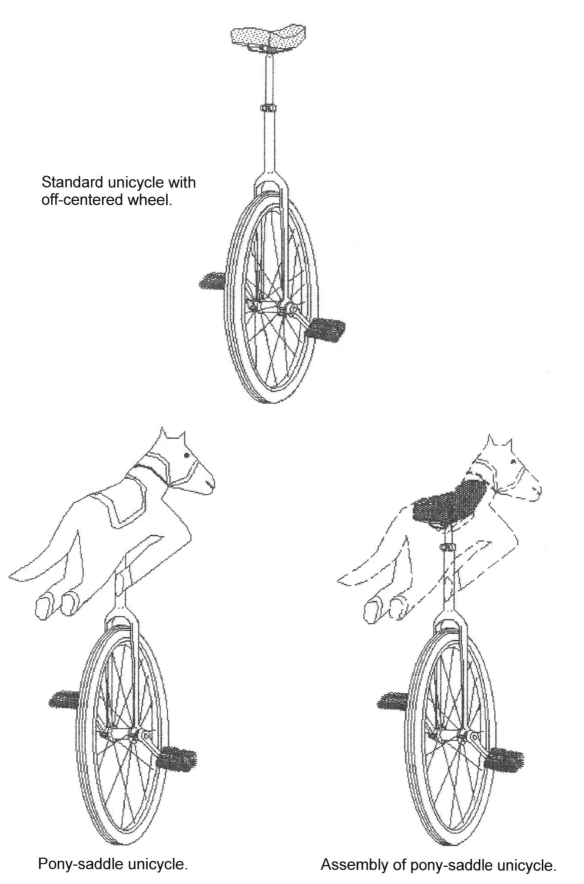

Standard unicycle with off-centered wheel.

Pony-saddle unicycle.

Assembly of pony-saddle unicycle.

39

STANDARD UNICYCLE WITH HANDLEBARS

A standard unicycle can be constructed with handlebars instead of a saddle. These can be ridden standing holding onto handlebar grips or sitting forward or backwards on the handlebars. A basic standard unicycle can be converted to a unicycle of this type by removing the saddle and saddle post and replacing them with a bicycle gooseneck and handlebars. The gooseneck is installed in the fork stem with an expansion bolt. A saddle-post clamp can be used for added support.

Another type of standard unicycle with handlebars has both a saddle and handlebars, as shown. Construction is by clamping or welding the handlebar unit to a basic standard unicycle.

If the standard unicycle developed from the penny farthing, the first unicycles probably had not only big wheels, but also handlebars. An 1896 sketch from a cycle show details a unicycle of this type.

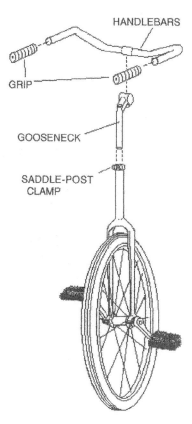

Adding handlebars to standard unicycle.

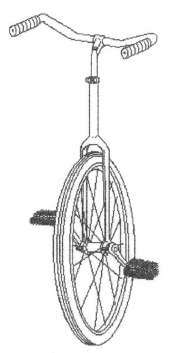

Standard unicycle with handlebars instead of saddle.

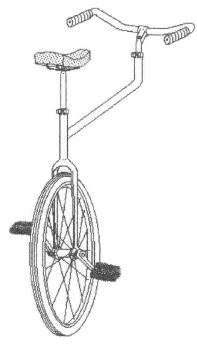

Standard unicycle with saddle and handlebars.

40

An 1896 sketch of a big-wheel unicycle with handlebars.

STANDARD UNICYCLE WITH POST

A standard unicycle can be constructed with a post instead of a saddle. A section of steel tubing with half the length of a saddle post inserted in one end and welded in place can be used to convert a standard uni-

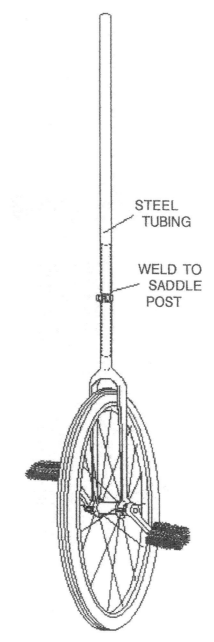

STEEL TUBING

WELD TO SADDLE POST

Standard unicycle with post instead of saddle.

An 1896 sketch of post unicycle.

cycle to a post model. The post is then held in place on the unicycle with the saddle post clamp. A post can be attached to a split-frame unicycle with the saddle post bolted in position in a similar manner.

An 1896 sketch shows a unicycle of this type.

41

DICYCLE

A dicycle has two wheels mounted on a common axis. A standard unicycle can be constructed with this wheel arrangement. An axle about 10 inches long is used. Two hubs or four flange washers are welded to the axle in a manner similar to that used for constructing a basic standard unicycle, as detailed previously in this chapter.

A wide fork is required for the dicycle. This can be constructed by adding an extension piece to a bicycle fork or made from stock materials.

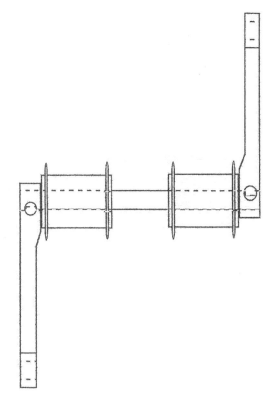

Hub and axle assembly for dicycle standard unicycle.

ULTIMATE WHEEL

An ultimate wheel is a unicycle wheel with pedal arms and pedals, but no frame or saddle. The name "ultimate wheel" is used because of the difficulty in learning to ride one.

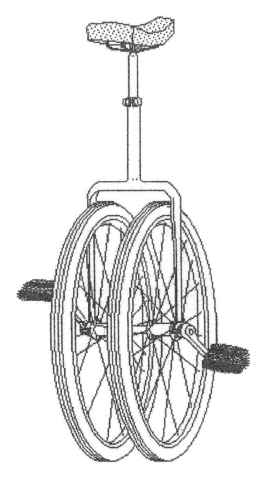

A dicycle unicycle with two parallel wheels attached to a common axle.

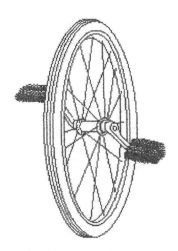

Ultimate wheel.

One possibility for an ultimate wheel is to remove the wheel assembly from a standard unicycle. However, while these have been ridden, it is usually easier if the pedals are closer to the center line. You can construct one in a manner similar to a standard unicycle wheel assembly, as detailed above in this chapter, except that a shorter axle is used with the crank arms mounted close to the hub flanges without bearings, as shown.

An 1896 sketch of a big-wheel ultimate wheel.

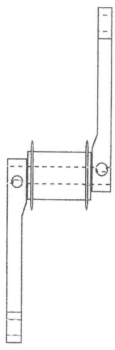

Hub and axle assembly for ultimate wheel.

Ultimate wheels were constructed and ridden before 1900. Shown are an 1896 sketch of a big-wheel ultimate wheel; one with a standard wheel; and one with a spiked wheel (definitely not recommended for inexperienced riders).

Somewhat easier to ride is a dicycle ultimate wheel. The hub and axle assembly is shown.

Some builders prefer to make the wheel or wheel centers from plywood rather than using a hubs and spokes. Metal plates with

An 1896 sketch of ultimate wheel with standard wheel.

An 1896 sketch of ultimate wheel with spikes.

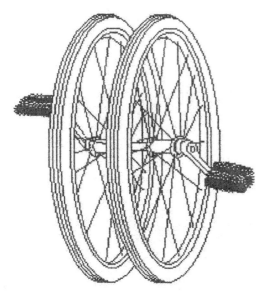

Dicycle ultimate wheel has two parallel wheels on a common axle.

threaded holes for the pedals are bolted to the plywood. Cutouts are made so that the metal plates are flush with the surface of the plywood. A bicycle rim can be mounted to the plywood with screws. A cutout is made in the plywood for the valve stem. The two wheels for a dicycle are attached to wood separating blocks. A rim liner, tube, and tire can then be mounted on the rim.

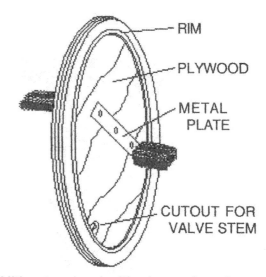

Ultimate wheel with plywood center.

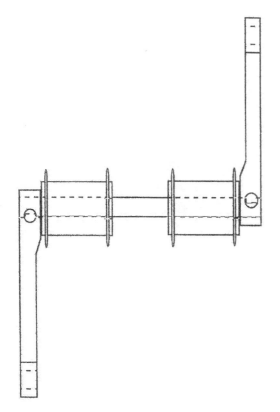

Hub and axle assembly for dicycle ultimate wheel.

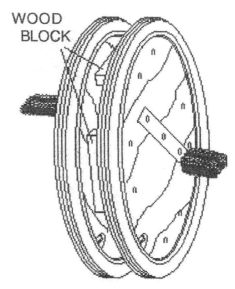

Dicycle ultimate wheel with plywood centers.

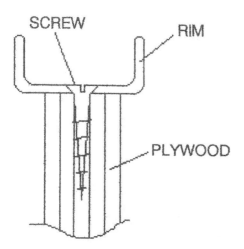

Rim is attached to plywood with screws.

IDEAS FOR OTHER STANDARD UNI-CYCLES

A variety of other novelty variations of the standard unicycle can be constructed, including a model with feet instead of a wheel; with out-of-round and square wheels; and even a half of wheel, which is ridden by bouncing over the missing half of the wheel.

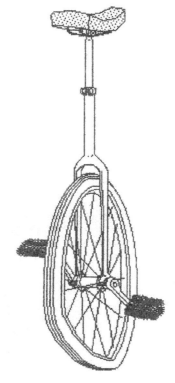

Standard unicycle with out-of-round wheel.

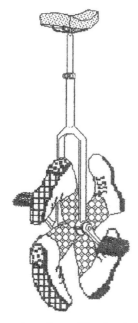

Standard unicycle with feet instead of wheel.

An 1896 sketch of handlebar unicycle with out-of-round wheel.

Standard unicycle with square wheel.   Standard unicycle with half a wheel.

An 1896 sketch of handle-
bar unicycle with square
wheel.

Chapter 5

HANDLEBAR UNITS AND UNIBIKES

Handlebar units, which can be constructed for use with standard or giraffe unicycles, and break-apart and unibikes are fun additions to unicycling.

HANDLEBAR UNIT FOR STANDARD UNICYCLE

Handlebar units for use with standard unicycles are shown. These units are not manufactured. However, the construction is easy and no welding is required.

Completed handlebar unit.

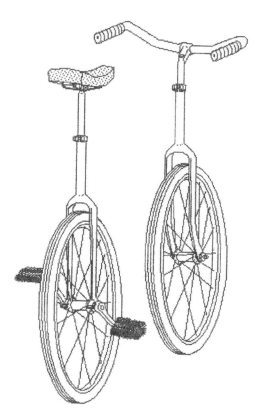

Handlebar unit for use with standard unicycle.

The assembly is shown. The wheel size on the handlebar unit is often the same size as that of the unicycle that it is used with, although other wheel sizes can also be used. In any case, you will need a bicycle fork that will fit the wheel that is to be used on the handlebar unit. Cut all but 1/4 inch of the threaded portion off the fork stem. If the finish on the fork is not in good condition, it can be painted at this time. Or you can have it chrome plated.

The component parts are shown ready for assembly.

A top fork nut is installed over the remaining threads on the fork handle. The handlebars are held in the fork with a standard bicycle gooseneck, as shown. The handlebar grips should be glued to the handlebars. Fasten front bicycle wheel assembly in place to complete the project.

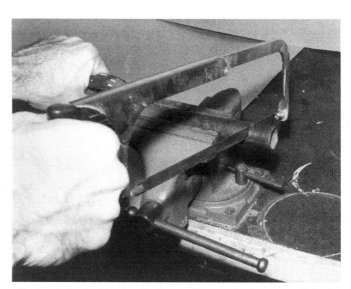

Cut all but 1/4 inch from threaded part of fork handle.

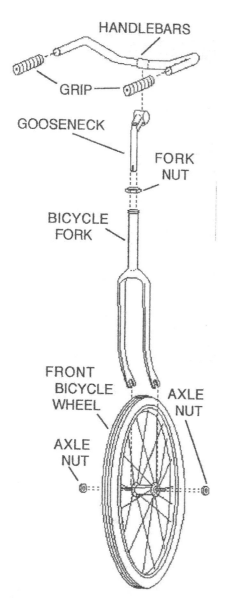

Assembly of handlebar unit.

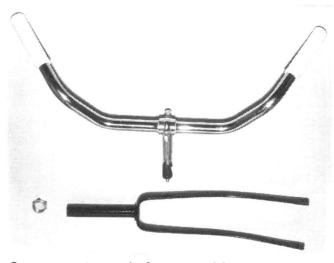

Components ready for assembly.

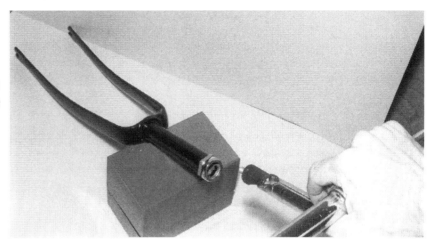

Handlebars are held in fork stem with bicycle gooseneck.

HANDLEBAR UNIT FOR GIRAFFE UNICYCLE

A handlebar unit for use with a giraffe unicycle is shown. Construction is similar to a unit for a standard unicycle, except that a section of tubing the same diameter and wall thickness as that of the fork stem is brazed or welded to the fork stem. The length of the extension will vary, depending on the height of the giraffe unicycle it will be used with. The handlebars of the finished unit should be about the same height as the unicycle saddle. The handlebars are fastened in the top end of the extension tubing with a standard bicycle gooseneck.

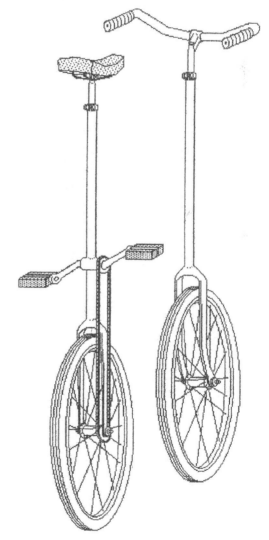

Handlebar unit for use with giraffe unicycle.

49

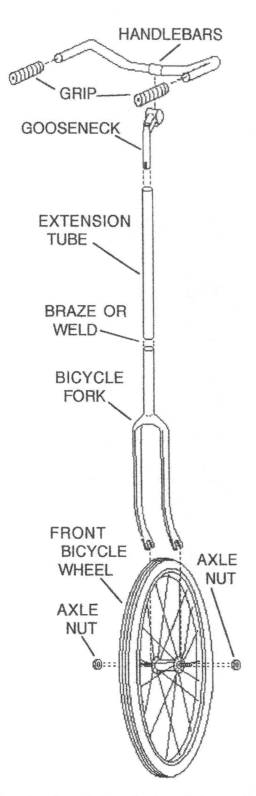

HANDLEBARS

GRIP

GOOSENECK

EXTENSION
TUBE

BRAZE OR
WELD

BICYCLE
FORK

FRONT
BICYCLE
WHEEL

AXLE
NUT

AXLE
NUT

Construction details for handlebar unit
for use with giraffe unicycle.

BREAK-APART UNITS

There are many possible variations for
break-apart units. Various links, such as
paper, elastic cords, or flexible rubber tubing, can be used to form a mock-up bicycle
from a unicycle and a handlebar unit.

Slip-apart metal linkages can be used to
form a break-apart bicycle from a standard
unicycle and a handle-bar unit.

The idea of break-apart bicycles dates
back to before 1900. An 1896 sketch shows
a penny farthing that slips apart to form an
ultimate wheel and another one illustrates a
bicycle with the rear wheel basically a
standard unicycle with slip-apart front
wheel, fork, and handlebars.

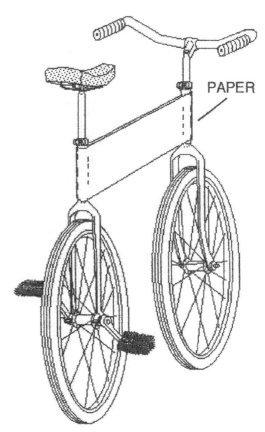

PAPER

Paper is used to connect standard unicycle and handlebar unit to form mock-
up bicycle.

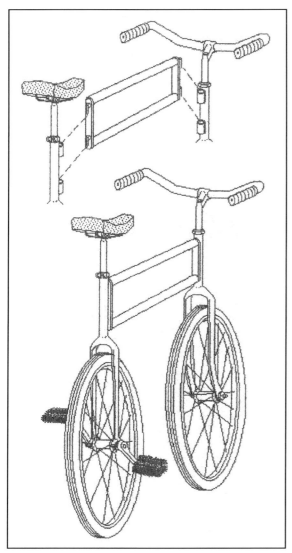

Slip-apart linkages and frame form break-apart bicycle from standard unicycle and handlebar unit.

An 1896 sketch of a penny farthing that slips apart to form an ultimate wheel.

An 1896 sketch of slip-apart bicycle.

A second basic type of break-apart bicycle forms two unicycles, each with its own rider. One version has a break-apart link between a standard unicycle with a saddle and a standard unicycle with handlebars instead of a saddle. Another version is similar, except that the front section also has a saddle. These cycles can be ridden as a bicycle with two riders, then break apart into two unicycles each with its own rider. This has good possibilities for comedy in a cycling stage act.

Regardless of the type constructed, a head tube and bearing assembly from a bicycle is used on the front fork so that the cycle will turn. For the version that has a saddle in front, the saddle mountings are brazed or welded to wheel well of the fork so that the fork can still turn in the head tube. A quick-release bolt is sometimes used to secure the sections during riding as a bicycle.

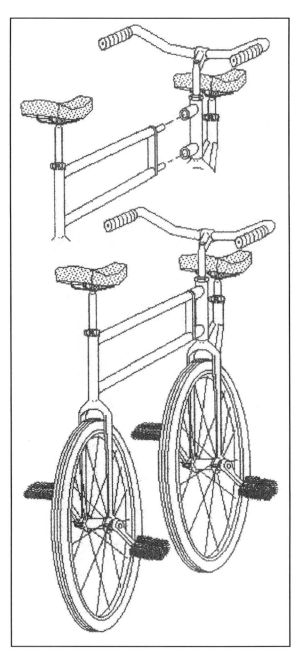

Break-apart bike with standard unicycle with saddle and standard unicycle with handlebars and saddle.

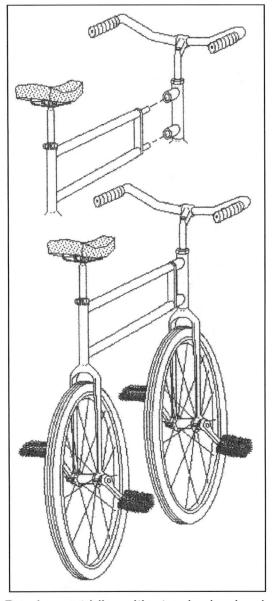

Break-apart bike with standard unicycle with saddle and standard unicycle with handlebars.

UNIBIKE

A unibike has a standard unicycle and handlebar unit connected to form a bicycle. The units can pivot at the head tube only or at both the seat tube and head tube. While the construction can be by means of tubing that fits over the fork handles without bearings, the use of a bicycle head tubes with the bearings and retainers will improve the performance.

While unibikes have usually been constructed from standard unicycles, these can also be constructed from giraffe unicycles.

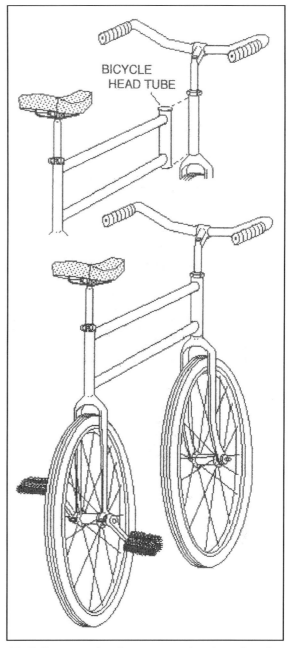

Unibike made from standard unicycle and handlebar unit with pivot at handlebar tube only.

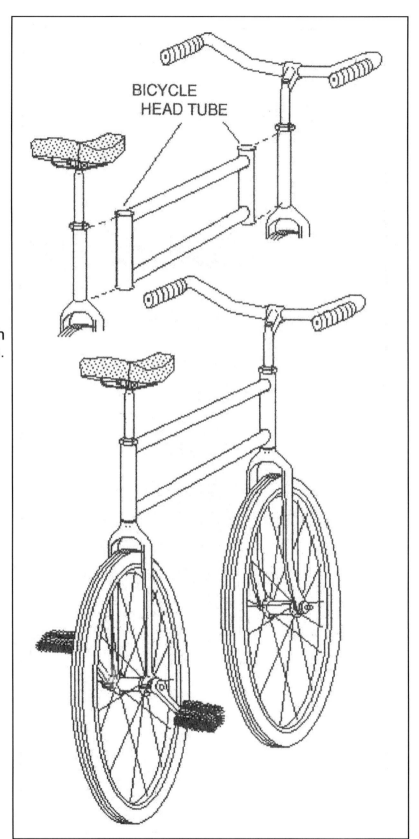

BICYCLE
HEAD TUBE

Unibike with pivots at both saddle and handlebar tubes.

Chapter 6

BUILDING GIRAFFE UNICYCLES

Giraffe unicycles have cranks above the drive wheel and a chain or other linkage to turn the wheel. The construction of what might be considered a basic giraffe unicycle is detailed first. These unicycles have a chain drive, measure from about four to six feet from the ground to the top of the saddle, and usually have 20-inch, 24-inch, or 26-inch wheels. Giraffe unicycles of other heights and wheel sizes and a number of novelty variations are then covered.

BASIC CHAIN-DRIVEN GIRAFFE UNICYCLE

A used bicycle will provide most of the parts for building a chain-driven giraffe unicycle of the type shown. The following parts are required:

- Section cut from a bicycle frame with crank assembly and saddle-post housing.
- Saddle post.
- Saddle-post clamp.
- Bicycle fork.
- Pedals (two required).
- Section of 1-inch inside diameter steel tubing (length varies depending on unicycle).
- Hub assembly with fixed sprocket.
- Spokes, rim, rim liner, tube, and tire.
- Chain (length varies depending on distance between sprockets and size of sprockets).
- Small sprocket that matches wheel sprocket.
- Unicycle saddle.

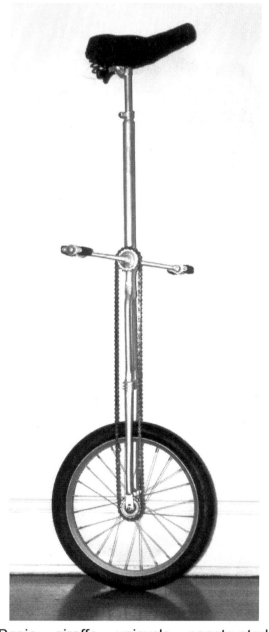

Basic giraffe unicycle constructed mostly from bicycle parts.

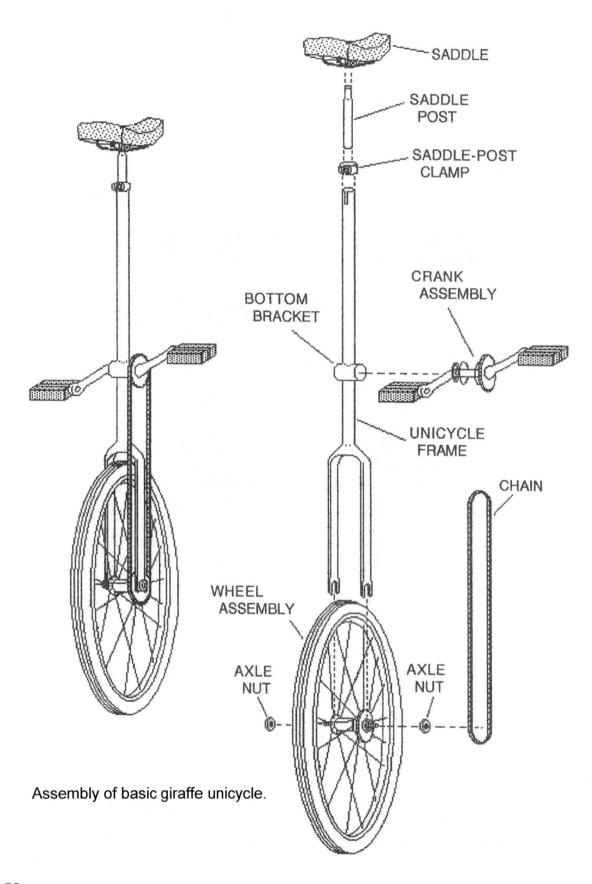

SADDLE

SADDLE POST

SADDLE-POST CLAMP

CRANK ASSEMBLY

BOTTOM BRACKET

UNICYCLE FRAME

CHAIN

WHEEL ASSEMBLY

AXLE NUT

AXLE NUT

Assembly of basic giraffe unicycle.

Wheel Assembly

A chain-driven unicycle requires a sprocket that is mounted solid with the hub, as detailed in Chapter 3. The hum is spoked to a rim of the desired wheel size, as detailed in Chapter 2. After aligning rim, install rim liner, tube, and tire to complete the wheel assembly.

Frame Assembly

Giraffe unicycle frames can be constructed from section cut from bicycle frames or stock materials. The construction of giraffe unicycle frames from sections of bicycles are shown. The first method shown requires a bicycle frame that is straight from the crank holders to the rear wheel. Regardless of the method used, straighten a fork from a bicycle of the same wheel size to be used on the unicycle. Methods for straightening forks are detailed in Chapter 2. A photo of a giraffe unicycle frame ready for brazing or welding is shown. The frame is brazed or welded to form a unit.

Saddle-post sections (seat tubes) cut from bicycle frames already have notches for saddle-post clamps. If a stock tube section was used, cut a 1-inch long, 3/16-inch wide notch in the upper rear of the frame for the saddle-post clamp.

In most cases, it will be necessary to widen the wheel-axle notches to take the larger rear axle (most bicycles have smaller front axles).

Grind and file the unicycle frame as required. The frame can then be painted or chrome plated, as desired.

Crank Assembly

The bicycle chainwheel is usually replaced with a sprocket that matches the one on the wheel hub for a one-to-one gear ratio, although other sizes and gear ratios will also work. Methods for installing small sprockets on cranks are detailed in Chapter 3. It is important to have the sprocket centered and aligned. After the sprocket has been brazed or welded in place, reassemble the crank in the bottom bracket with bicycle grease applied to the bearings. Install pedals.

Chain

Use only heavy duty chain and make certain it is in good condition. Methods for lengthening and shortening chains are detailed in Chapter 2. Make chain connections as necessary so that the chain is the correct length to fit the unicycle. Fasten the wheel assembly in place and adjust until the chain is tight. Slack in the chain causes play in the pedal action and makes the unicycle much more difficult to ride.

Saddle

Any of the unicycle saddles detailed in Chapter 3 can be used on a giraffe unicycle. The saddle post is held in the unicycle frame with a standard bicycle saddle-post clamp. This completes the construction of a basic chain-drive unicycle.

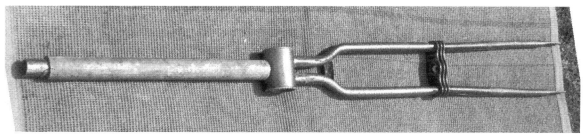

Giraffe unicycle frame ready for brazing or welding.

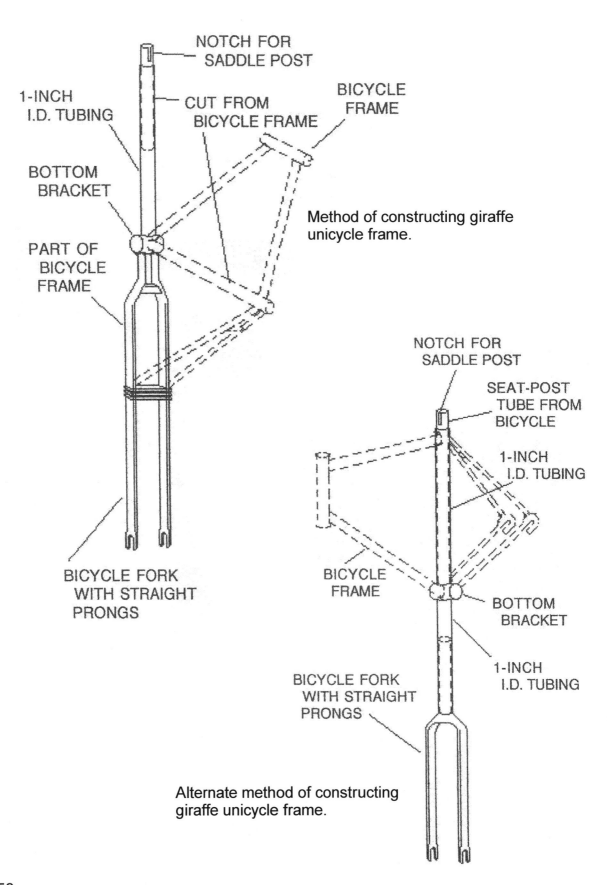

NOTCH FOR SADDLE POST

1-INCH I.D. TUBING

CUT FROM BICYCLE FRAME

BICYCLE FRAME

BOTTOM BRACKET

Method of constructing giraffe unicycle frame.

PART OF BICYCLE FRAME

BICYCLE FORK WITH STRAIGHT PRONGS

NOTCH FOR SADDLE POST

SEAT-POST TUBE FROM BICYCLE

1-INCH I.D. TUBING

BICYCLE FRAME

BOTTOM BRACKET

1-INCH I.D. TUBING

BICYCLE FORK WITH STRAIGHT PRONGS

Alternate method of constructing giraffe unicycle frame.

SHORT MODEL

A chain-driven giraffe unicycle can be made shorter by placing the bottom bracket closer to the wheel well, as shown.

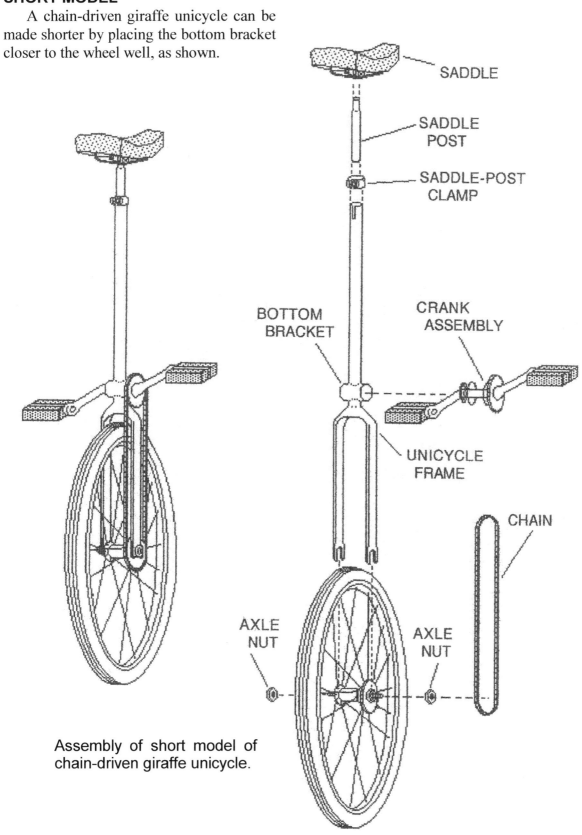

Assembly of short model of chain-driven giraffe unicycle.

SMALL WHEEL

Chain-driven unicycles can also be constructed with smaller wheels, such as the 12-inch wheel model shown. The assembly of a small-wheel giraffe is illustrated.

Small-wheel giraffe unicycles often use a larger sprocket at the crank than at the wheel to give a pedal action similar to a giraffe unicycle with a larger wheel.

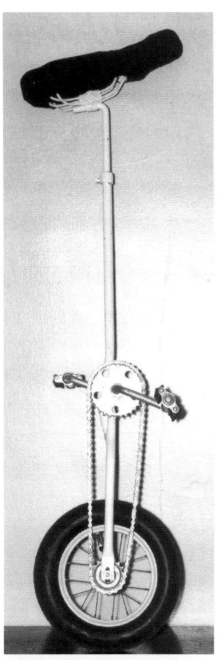

Chain-driven giraffe unicycle with 12-inch wheel.

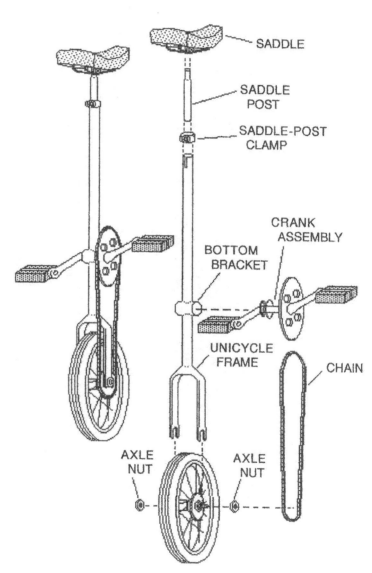

Assembly of giraffe unicycle with small wheel.

TINY WHEEL

Chain-driven giraffe unicycles called "tiny-wheel" models can be constructed with wheels 3 inches or even smaller in diameter. A heavy duty caster wheel with a metal center can be used. Use a spacer between the hub and sprocket and bolt or braze or weld the sprocket and spacer to the metal wheel hub. A large chainwheel and a small sprocket at the wheel hub is almost essential for a tiny-wheel unicycle.

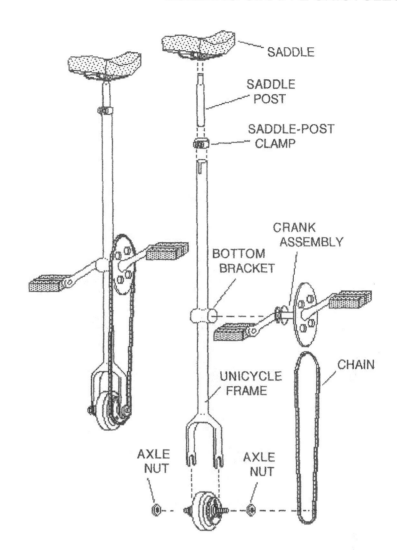

Assembly of tiny-wheel giraffe unicycle.

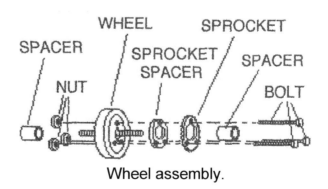

Wheel assembly.

BIG WHEEL

Giraffe unicycles can be constructed with large diameter wheels, as shown. Use a large sprocket at the wheel hub and a small sprocket at the cranks to give a pedal action similar to that of a basic chain-driven giraffe unicycle.

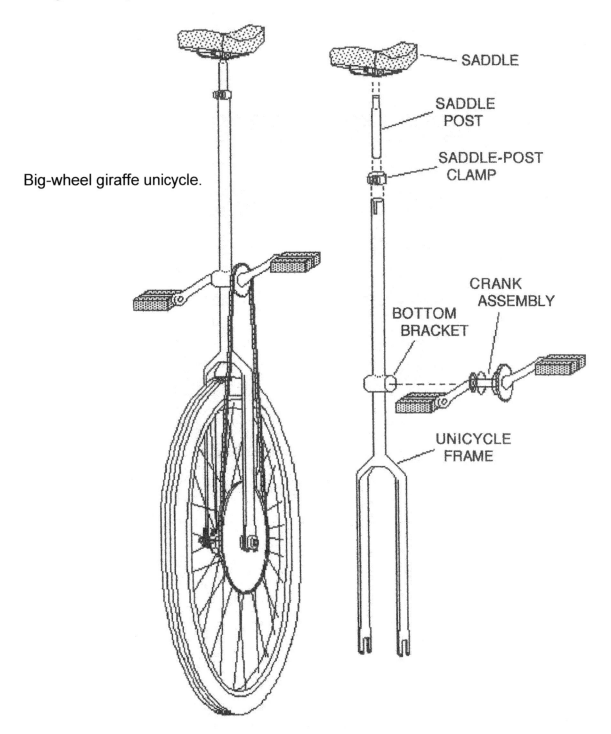

Big-wheel giraffe unicycle.

SADDLE

SADDLE POST

SADDLE-POST CLAMP

CRANK ASSEMBLY

BOTTOM BRACKET

UNICYCLE FRAME

TALL UNICYCLES

Unicycles up to about 10-feet tall can be constructed as detailed above in this chapter for 4 to 6-foot models, except the construction should be stronger. For unicycles over about 8-feet tall, it is advisable to use sprockets on both sides and two chains.

On extremely tall models, the unicycle frame should be well reinforced. One way to do this and still keep the weight down to reasonable limits is to use lattice-type reinforcing members made of steel tubing and/or rod.

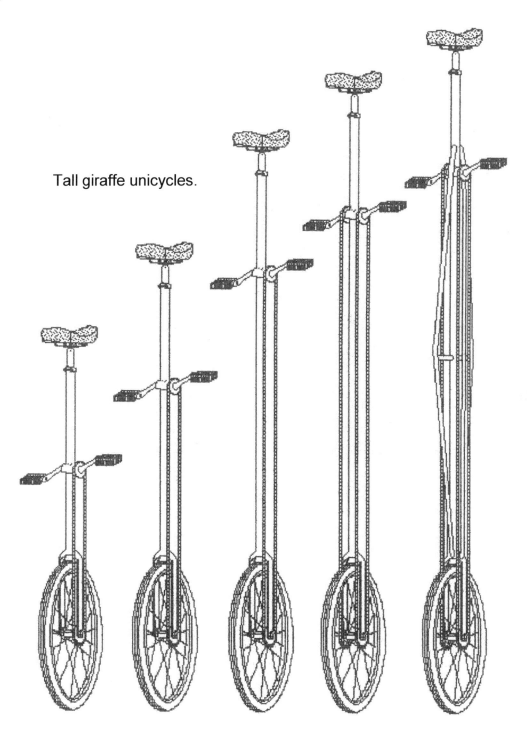

Tall giraffe unicycles.

ZIGZAG FRAMES

Chain-driven giraffe unicycles can be constructed with zigzag frames. A sturdy frame construction is required. Double connected sprockets are used at the bends and separate chains are used to link each straight section from the wheel to the crank. Many different frame variations are possible for zigzag unicycles.

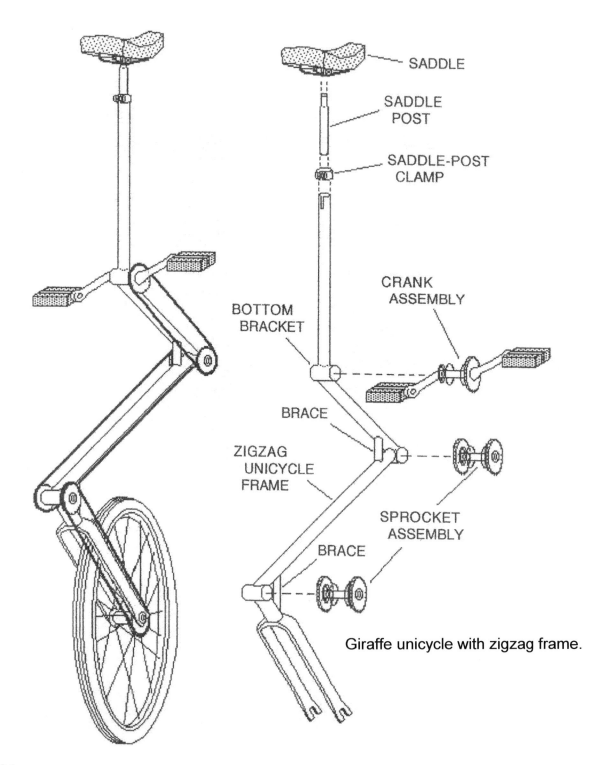

SADDLE

SADDLE POST

SADDLE-POST CLAMP

BOTTOM BRACKET

CRANK ASSEMBLY

BRACE

ZIGZAG UNICYCLE FRAME

SPROCKET ASSEMBLY

BRACE

Giraffe unicycle with zigzag frame.

Zigzag unicycles have also been constructed with the bends to the sides rather than forward and backwards. One version has the chains parallel to each other and perpendicular to the dual-sprocket shaft.

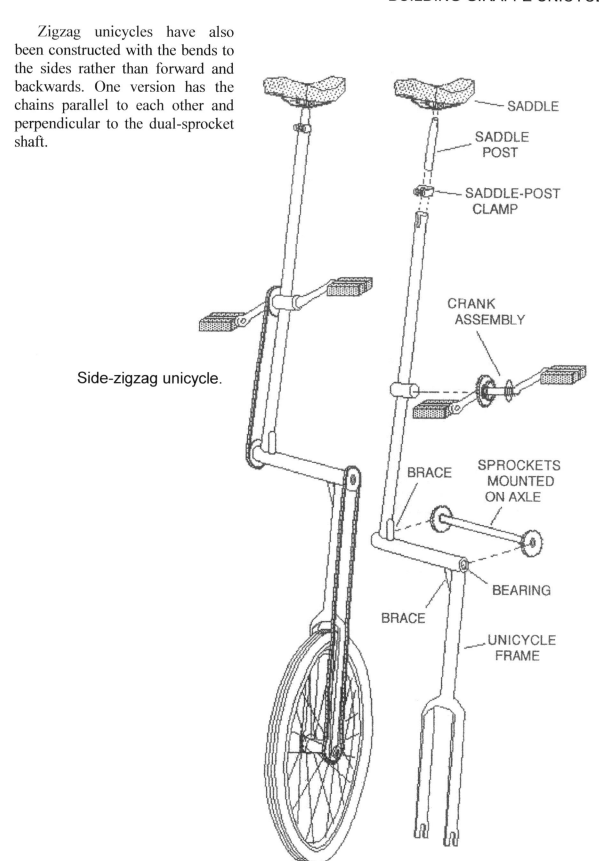

Side-zigzag unicycle.

SADDLE

SADDLE POST

SADDLE-POST CLAMP

CRANK ASSEMBLY

BRACE

SPROCKETS MOUNTED ON AXLE

BEARING

BRACE

UNICYCLE FRAME

Another version of the side-zigzag unicycle uses universal joints in the dual-sprocket shaft so that the cross frame does not need to be parallel to the sprockets.

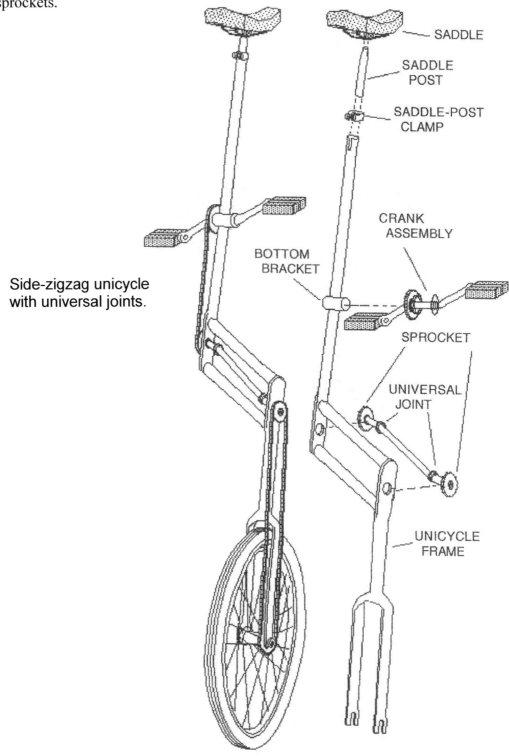

Side-zigzag unicycle with universal joints.

SADDLE

SADDLE POST

SADDLE-POST CLAMP

CRANK ASSEMBLY

BOTTOM BRACKET

SPROCKET

UNIVERSAL JOINT

UNICYCLE FRAME

MULTI-WHEEL GIRAFFE UNICYCLES

Giraffe unicycles can be constructed with more than one wheel. One type has a chain drive, with the extra wheels turning for decorative purposes. The two decorative wheels are mounted so that the drive wheel will cause them to turn. Another type has the wheels turning each other without a chain drive. If three wheels are used, the direction the crank turns is the same as the direction the ground wheel turns. The upper section of this type unicycle is essentially a standard unicycle, as detailed in Chapter 4. The lower portion consists of two fork-prong extensions that allow upward and downward adjustment of the two lower wheels. The three wheels can be the same size, or the center wheel can be smaller or larger than the other two without changing the one-to-one drive ratio. The lower and upper wheels can be of different sizes, but this will change the drive ratio.

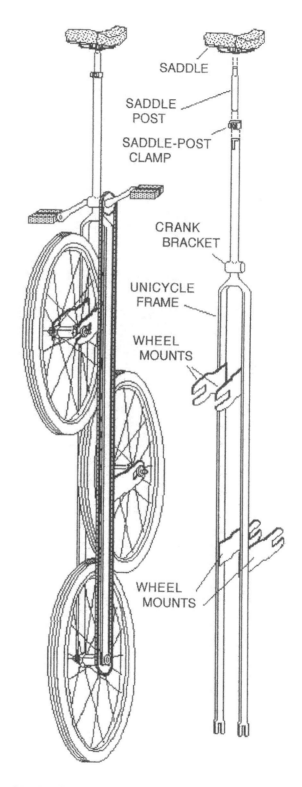

SADDLE

SADDLE POST

SADDLE-POST CLAMP

CRANK BRACKET

UNICYCLE FRAME

WHEEL MOUNTS

WHEEL MOUNTS

Chain-driven giraffe unicycle with decorative wheels.

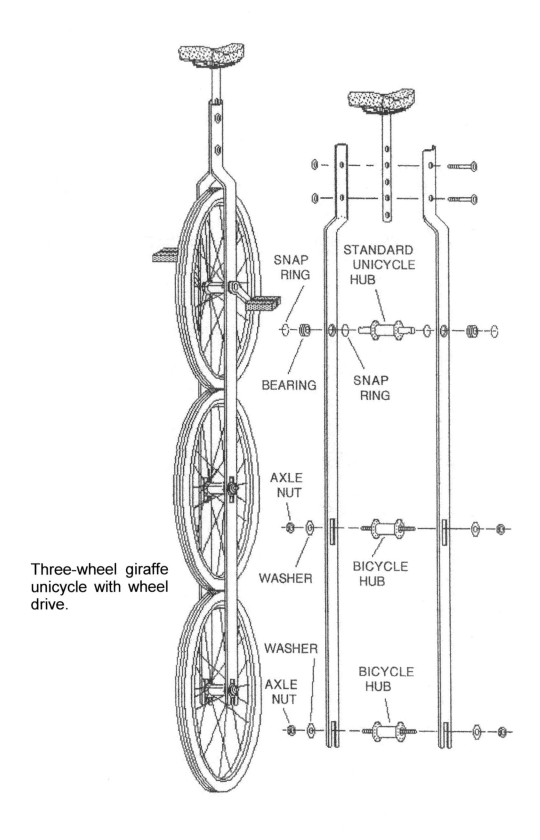

SNAP RING

STANDARD UNICYCLE HUB

BEARING

SNAP RING

AXLE NUT

BICYCLE HUB

Three-wheel giraffe unicycle with wheel drive.

WASHER

WASHER

AXLE NUT

BICYCLE HUB

A giraffe unicycle with five wheels can be constructed in a similar manner. Even more wheels can be added. A thirteen wheeler, which I believe is the record number to date, is shown.

If two wheels are used, the ground wheel will turn in the opposite direction of the crank, making riding extremely diffi- cult and challenging. When you pedal forward, the lower wheel turns backward. A few people have actually learned to ride these. Construction is similar to a three-wheel model, with the exception of shorter fork prongs and one less wheel. Similar cycles can also be constructed with four or six wheels.

Thirteen-wheel giraffe unicycle (courtesy Jack Halpern and the Japan Unicycle Association).

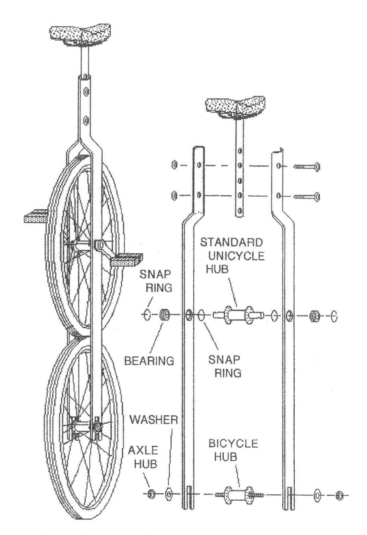

Two-wheel giraffe unicycle with wheel drive.

A two wheeler with a half wheel at the cranks is another unusual design. A unicycle of this type has been built and successfully ridden.

A two-wheel model can be constructed to give the normal pedal direction by using a reversing gear at the cranks.

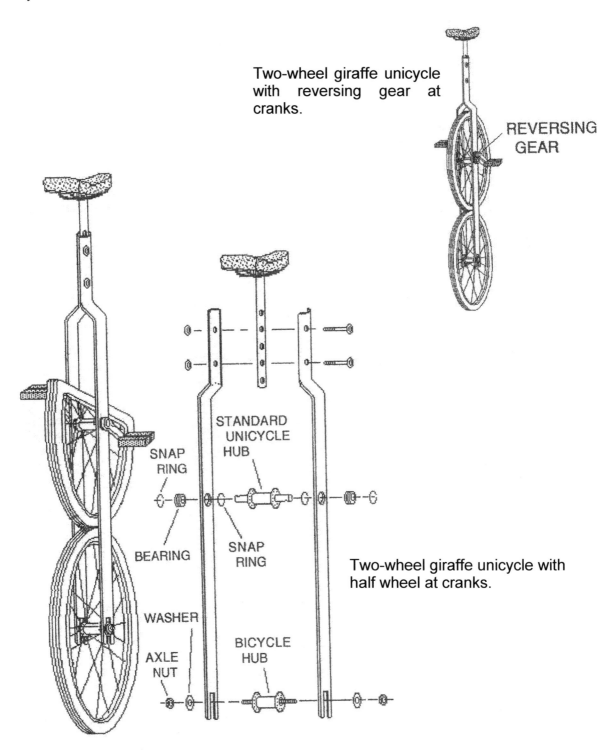

Two-wheel giraffe unicycle with reversing gear at cranks.

REVERSING GEAR

STANDARD UNICYCLE HUB

SNAP RING

BEARING

SNAP RING

Two-wheel giraffe unicycle with half wheel at cranks.

WASHER

AXLE NUT

BICYCLE HUB

TANDEM CHAIN-DRIVEN UNICYCLES

At least two basic designs of tandem unicycles have been constructed. One design, which has proven difficult to ride, has one rider forward of the wheel and the other being the wheel. Another type has one rider above the other rider.

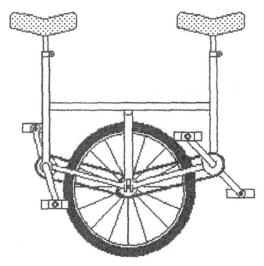

Chain-driven tandem unicycle with saddles in line.

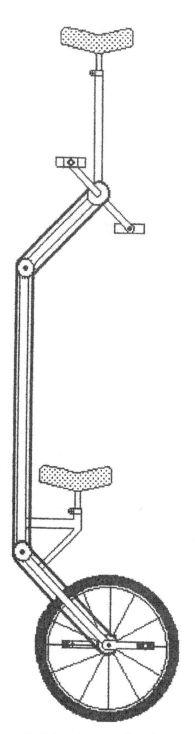

Tall tandem unicycle.

Chapter 7

ARTISTIC AND NOVELTY BICYCLES

Construction of artistic bicycles is detailed first. This is followed by a section on the construction of other novelty bicycles, including one with off-centered wheels.

ARTISTIC BICYCLES

Artistic bicycles are special bicycles that have a fixed rear hub sprocket (no freewheeling) and usually a one-to-one drive ratio. This allows pedaling forward or backwards and riding on the rear wheel alone like a unicycle. Artistic bicycles often also have straight (no rake) front forks and saddles that curve upward at the rear and are mounted further toward the rear of the cycle than is normal for a regular bicycle. Other important features include having the seat tube and bottom bracket close to the rear wheel and that the cycle is lightweight. Many artistic bicycles also have axle extensions for use as foot stands, which make additional stunts possible.

While many standard bicycles can be converted to workable artistic bicycles, some are more suitable than others. An artistic bicycle of the type used in international competition is shown.

Direct-drive bicycle that can be ridden on real wheel like a chain -driven unicycle.

Artistic bicycle.

Frames

A variety of bicycle frames can be modified for use on artistic bicycles. A track racing bicycle with short rear stays can be used without modifications to the basic frame. Other frames will require shortening of the rear stays so that the rear wheel will be mounted closer to the seat stay and bottom bracket. A frame that has been shortened is shown. The frame selected should also be lightweight, sturdy, and for the wheel size that you intend to use (usually 26 or 27-inch wheels for adults, but 20 and 24-inch sizes can also be used; smaller riders often prefer the smaller

wheel sizes).

Artistic bicycles usually have front forks with straight (no rake) prongs. Methods for straightening fork prongs are detailed in Chapter 2. It is advisable to use a front wheel with a larger than normal axle diameter, usually the same size as that of the rear axle. The axle notches in the fork prongs will need to be widened to fit a larger axle. The frame and assembly of an artistic bicycle is shown.

The artistic bicycle frame can be painted or chrome plated, as desired.

Wheel Assemblies

A regular front bicycle wheel can be used for the front wheel of the artistic bicycle. However, it is advisable to replace the standard hub with one with a larger diameter axle. This is especially important if axle extensions or dorns are to be used, as detailed below in this section.

The rear wheel requires a fixed sprocket. Methods for constructing fixed sprocket hubs are given in Chapter 3. It is important to have the spoked rim centered in the bicycle frame and the fixed sprocket aligned with the crank sprocket.

Competition-type artistic bicycle.

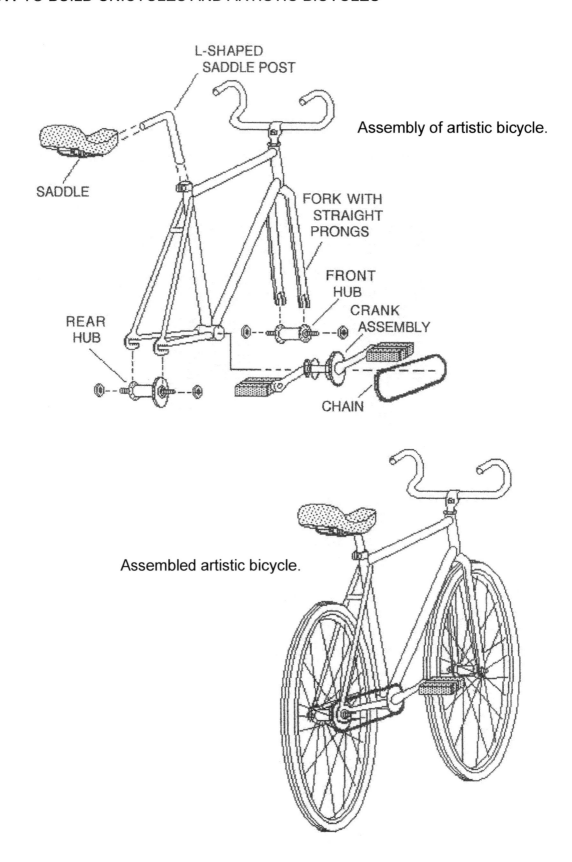

L-SHAPED
SADDLE POST

Assembly of artistic bicycle.

SADDLE

FORK WITH
STRAIGHT
PRONGS

FRONT
HUB

CRANK
ASSEMBLY

REAR
HUB

CHAIN

Assembled artistic bicycle.

Steel tube extension or dorns can be threaded onto the ends of the axles for use as foot stands. The extensions are usually about an inch long. They make additional stunts possible.

Crank Assembly and Chain

Shorter crank arms are generally used on an artistic bicycle than on a regular bicycle, although the exact length is largely a matter of personal preference. The standard front chainwheel is usually replaced with a small sprocket that matches the one on the rear hub. This will give a one-to-one drive ratio. Competition artistic bicycles generally use sprockets with 24 teeth. Methods for installing small sprockets on cranks are detailed in Chapter 3.

The chain length will usually need to be shortened for use on the artistic bicycle. The chain length should allow for adjusting the chain tension by positioning the rear axle in the bracket slot.

Handlebars

A variety of handlebars are suitable for use on artistic bicycles. Racing and touring bicycle handlebars are often used on artistic bicycles. These are usually turned upward, as shown. A standard bicycle gooseneck can be used for mounting the handlebars to the fork stem. However, a gooseneck that has the handlebar mounting directly above or as close as possible to the mounting shaft is recommended, as this will place the handlebars over the front wheel center in both wheel directions. If handlebar grips are used, they should be cemented in place so they will not slip.

Saddles

The saddle should curve upward at the rear and be positioned further toward the rear of the bicycle than is a regular bicycle saddle. One possibility is to use a banana-type saddle, as shown.

Competition-type artistic bicycles use a saddle of the shape shown. The rear of the saddle curves upward and widens outward. Some standard bicycle saddles can be modified to this shape.

An L-shaped saddle post can be used for mounting the saddle to the bicycle frame. This arrangement allows mounting the saddle further toward the rear of the cycle. Braces that attach to the upper rear stays on the bicycle frame are sometimes added to the back of the saddle.

NOVELTY BICYCLES

There are a number of other novelty bicycles that can be used in shows, acts, demonstrations, parade riding, and so on.

Small Wheel Bicycles

Small wheel bicycles that convert to giraffe unicycles or other forms are popular, such as with a removable saddle and post with a quick-release bolt that can be switched to a bracket on the head tube to form the saddle of a giraffe unicycle. These cycles have the crank and drive system similar to an artistic bicycle, except that a chainwheel larger than the hub sprocket is usually used.

Off-Centered Wheels

A popular novelty bicycle is one with off-centered wheels. This can be a regular bicycle or an artistic bicycle of the type detailed above. Methods for spoking off-centered wheels are detailed in Chapter 3. In most cases, it will be necessary to use a smaller wheel size than was used on the bicycle being converted to give adequate wheel-well clearance for the tires. It may also be necessary to use shorter crank arms to give adequate ground clearance for the pedals.

Bicycle with off-centered wheels.

Miniature Bicycles

Two basic types of miniature bicycles are popular: those that are ridden sitting on a saddle and those that are ridden standing on the pedals in a squat position. The challenge is to construct a bicycle as small as possible that can still be ridden. The construction can be a real engineering and machining challenge. The parts must be both tiny and strong, which is a difficult combination to achieve.

Other Possibilities

Other Possibilities include double-decker and tall bicycles, tandem bicycles for large numbers of riders, penny farthings and other early bicycle designs, and recumbent bicycles.

APPENDIX

SOURCES FOR UNICYCLES AND PARTS

Dube Juggling Equipment
www.dube.com
Offers unicycles and a complete line of juggling equipment.

Semcycle
www.semcycle.com
Manufactures and sells high quality standard and giraffe unicycles.

Sunrise Cyclery
www.sunrisecyclery.com
Unicycles are available in all sizes.

The Unicycle Factory
Tom Miller
2711 N. Apperson
Kokomo, IN 46901
Sells Zepher, Semcycle, and Miyata unicycles. Also sells parts and custom builds giraffe and a variety of novelty unicycles.

Unicycle Store
www.infiniteillusions.com
Sells a variety of standard and giraffe unicycles.

Unicycles on Sale
www.brandscycle.com
Sells Torker and Cycle Pro unicycles.

ORGANIZATIONS

International Unicycling Federation
www.unicycling.org/iuf
Sponsors world unicycling competitions.

Unicycling Society of America
www.unicycling.org/usa
Publishes a newsletter and sponsors national unicycling competitions.

INDEX

Aligning wheels, 10-12, 22
Artistic bicycles, 72-76
Assembly (of bicycles), 10
Axles, 15, 23-28, 38, 42-44

Basic standard unicycles, 23-34
Bearing holders, 28-33
Big-wheel unicycle, 37, 62
Break-apart units, 50-52
Building, reasons for, 5-6

Chain, 14, 57, 75
Chain-driven unicycle, 55-67, 71
Chain tool, 8, 14
Crank assemblies, 8, 17-20, 57, 75
Crank sprockets, 17-20
Cutting, 12

Dicycle, 42, 43-44
Disassembly (of bicycles), 10
Drill, 7-8
Drilling, 13
Double-decker bicycles, 75

Feet-wheel unicycle, 45
Filing, 13
Files, metal, 13
Flattening (tubing), 12
Fork prongs (straightening), 13
Frame assembly, 28-33, 37, 57, 58, 73-74

Giraffe unicycles, 55-71
Grinder, power, 13
Grinding, 13

Half-wheel, 45-46, 70
Handlebars, 40-41, 47-50, 75
Handlebar units, 47-50
Hubs, 15-17, 23-28, 39, 42, 43, 44

Kangaroo unicycle, 39

Lacing spokes, 10-12

Maintenance rack, 8
Materials, 5-6, 8-9
Midget unicycle, 34-36
Miniature bicycles, 75
Multi-wheel giraffe unicycles, 67-70

Novelty bicycles, 75-76

Off-centered wheel, 22, 38, 75-76
Organizations, 78
Out-of-round wheel, 45

Parts, 8-9, 77
Penny farthing, 23, 50-51, 75
Pipe cutter, 7
Pony-saddle unicycle, 38-39
Post unicycle, 41

Recumbent bicycle, 75

Saddle, artistic bicycle, 74, 75
Saddle, unicycle, 20-21, 33, 57
Short-model unicycle, 59
Side-zigzag unicycles, 64-66
Small-wheel unicycle, 34-36, 60
Spoke wrench, 8
Spoking wheels, 10-12, 22
Sprockets, 15-20
Square-wheel unicycles, 45-46
Standard unicycles, 23-46
Standard unicycle with handlebars, 40-41
Standard unicycle with post, 41

Tall bicycles, 75
Tall unicycles, 62
Tandem unicycles, 70
Tandem bicycles, 75
Tiny-wheel unicycle, 61

APPENDIX

Tire lever, 8
Tools, 7-8
Truing stand, 11

Ultimate wheel, 42-45
Unibike, 53-54
Unicycle parts, 77
Wheel alignment, 10-12, 22

Wheel assembly, 23-28, 57, 73
Wheel-truing stand, 11-12
Work areas, 7

Zigzag unicycles, 64-66

ABOUT THE AUTHOR

Jack Wiley has had a varied career. He traveled overland by buses and trains from the United States to Buenos Aires, Argentina, and returned by way of the Amazon; received his Ph.D. from the University of Illinois in 1968; did physiology research at the University of California at Santa Barbara; and lived aboard a sailboat for a number of years.

Dr. Jack Wiley first became interested in unicycling when he was in the seventh grade. A friend showed him the remains of a unicycle that had belonged to his uncle, a former professional stage performer. Jack Wiley purchased the unicycle and restored it with the help of a man at a bicycle shop.

He then learned to ride the unicycle, built other cycles, and worked up an amateur act. He performed in many shows in and around Fresno, California, including the Annual YMCA Circus.

Unicycling has remained an important part of his life since that time, and he has authored a number of books on the subject, including *How to Ride a Unicycle* and *The Complete Book of Unicycling*.

For more information about the author and his books, go to:

http://www.amazon.com/author/ jackwileypublications.

The author at an early age practicing for a YMCA circus.

Printed in Great Britain
by Amazon